REMOTE CAPTURE

Remote Capture

Digitising Documentary Heritage in Challenging Locations

Edited by
Jody Butterworth, Andrew Pearson,
Patrick Sutherland and Adam Farquhar

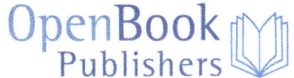

http://www.openbookpublishers.com

© 2018 Jody Butterworth, Andrew Pearson, Patrick Sutherland and Adam Farquhar.
Copyright of individual chapters is maintained by the chapter's author

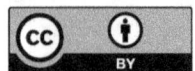

This work is licensed under a Creative Commons Attribution 4.0 International license (CC BY 4.0). This license allows you to share, copy, distribute and transmit the work; to adapt the work and to make commercial use of the work providing attribution is made to the authors (but not in any way that suggests that they endorse you or your use of the work). Attribution should include the following information:

Jody Butterworth, Andrew Pearson, Patrick Sutherland and Adam Farquhar (eds.), *Remote Capture: Digitising Documentary Heritage in Challenging Locations*. Cambridge, UK: Open Book Publishers, 2018. https://doi.org/10.11647/OBP.0138

In order to access detailed and updated information on the license, please visit https://www.openbookpublishers.com/product/747#copyright

Further details about CC BY licenses are available at http://creativecommons.org/licenses/by/4.0/

All external links were active at the time of publication otherwise stated and have been archived via the Internet Archive Wayback Machine at https://archive.org/web

Every effort has been made to identify and contact copyright holders and any omission or error will be corrected if notification is made to the publisher.

Digital material and resources associated with this volume are available at https://www.openbookpublishers.com/product/747#resources

Open Field Guides Series, vol. 1 | ISSN: 2514-2496 (Print); 2514 250X (Online)

ISBN Paperback: 978-1-78374-473-2
ISBN Hardback: 978-1-78374-474-9
ISBN Digital (PDF): 978-1-78374-475-6
ISBN Digital ebook (epub): 978-1-78374-476-3
ISBN Digital ebook (mobi): 978-1-78374-477-0
DOI: 10.11647/OBP.0138

The OBP team involved in the production of this book: Alessandra Tosi (managing editor), Lucy Barnes (editing and copyediting), Bianca Gualandi (layout and digital production) and Heidi Coburn (cover design).

Cover image: Monks digitising Buddhist manuscripts in a courtyard at Gangtey Monastery, Bhutan (2006). Photo by Karma Phuntsho, CC-BY 4.0.

All paper used by Open Book Publishers is SFI (Sustainable Forestry Initiative), and PEFC (Programme for the endorsement of Forest Certification Schemes) Certified.

Printed in the United Kingdom, United States and Australia
by Lightning Source for Open Book Publishers (Cambridge, UK).

Contents

List of figures	1
List of tables	5
Contributors	7
Foreword	9
Acknowledgements	11
A note on the text boxes	13
Brands and manufacturers	13
Digital resources	14
Introduction	15
1. Planning the project	19
Project design	19
Calculating the budget	25
2. Equipment and skills for digitising in the field	41
Cameras and scanners	41
The Digital SLR camera: a general introduction	45
DSLRs: principles and settings	47
Tripods, copy stands and remote controls	64
Lighting and flash	73
Copying glass plate negatives and transparencies	78
Essential equipment and skills	81

Practical advice for photography in the field	82
Hard drives and data management	86
Scanners	87

3. Image standards — 93
Introduction	93
Considerations	95
Examples of good and bad images	98

4. Collection care and document handling — 113
General considerations for safe handling of library material	113
Dirty and dusty material	115
Pictures and glass plate negatives	116
Loose-leaf items	116
Bound items	117
Housing	119

5. A workflow for digitisation — 121
Preparation	122
Creation of the digital images	126
Renaming and organising the digital images	128
Developing and exporting the digital images	129
Backing up	130
Virus checking	136
Cataloguing/creation of metadata	136

6. On the ground — 139
Before departure	141
Politics	148
Local liaison and partnerships	154
Managing expectations	154
Communication	159

    Staff and their management   160
    Money   164
    Outreach and publicity   167

Conclusion   171

Further resources   175
    Useful downloads   175
    Other reading   175
    Glossary   176

Index   179

Digital Appendices

Available online at https://doi.org/10.11647/OBP.0138.11
    Digital Appendix 1. Practical Methods for Digitisation
    Digital Appendix 2. Using Electronic Flash
    Digital Appendix 3. Digitisation Process Notes
    Digital Appendix 4. Costed Equipment List

List of figures

The copyright for the images reproduced in this book belongs to the individual EAP grant holders. However, as part of the Endangered Archives Programme conditions of award, grant holders give consent that EAP can share information submitted as part of a project. We would nevertheless like to thank all the EAP grant holders who have provided these photographs as part of their project archive. Drawn illustrations were produced by Anne Leaver.

1. EAP650, Archiving Afro-Colombian history in Caloto Viejo, Colombia. Photo © Thomas Desch Obi, CC BY 4.0. 10
2. EAP704, En route to Marawe Krestos, Ethiopia. Photo © Michael Gervers, CC BY 4.0. 12
3. EAP700, Preserving the manuscripts of the Jaffna Bishop's House, Sri Lanka. Photo © Appasamy Murugaiyan, CC BY 4.0. 14
4. EAP329, A peripatetic project digitising Acehnese manuscripts in rudimentary circumstances, Indonesia. Photo © Fakhriati Thahir, CC BY 4.0. 22
5. EAP039, Photographing Buddhist manuscripts in Bhutan. Photo © Karma Phuntsho, CC BY 4.0. 24
6. EAP524, The St Helena Government Archives, Jamestown. Photo © Andrew Pearson, CC BY 4.0. 29
7. EAP627, A fragile manuscript from Paraíba, Brazil. Photo © Courtney Campbell, CC BY 4.0. 31

8. EAP643, Manuscripts prepared for digitisation, Bengal.
   Photo © Abhijit Bhattacharya, CC BY 4.0. 34
9. EAP488, An EAP team in action, Mali.
   Photo © Sophie Sarin, CC BY 4.0. 35
10. EAP644, Camera and scanner used in parallel, Beirut.
    Photo © Yasmine Chemali, CC BY 4.0. 42
11. Example histograms.
    Photos © Patrick Sutherland, CC BY 4.0. 56
12. Greyscale and colour checker.
    Photo © Patrick Sutherland, CC BY 4.0. 58
13. EAP704 Däbrä Abbay and EAP526 May Wäyni, Ethiopia.
    Photo © Michael Gervers, CC BY 4.0. 58
14. Electronic grids assist with the alignment of objects when
    copying. Photo © Patrick Sutherland, CC BY 4.0. 63
15. EOS Utility. Photo © Patrick Sutherland, CC BY 4.0. 66
16. Copy stand with angled lights.
    Illustration © Anne Leaver, CC BY 4.0. 68
17. EAP524, Camera and copy stand in situ in the St Helena
    Government Archives.
    Photo © Andrew Pearson, CC BY 4.0. 68
18. Diagram of copy stand in reversed position.
    Illustration © Anne Leaver, CC BY 4.0. 69
19. EAP769, Digitising using a tripod with a central column in
    Montserrat. Photo © Nigel Sadler, CC BY 4.0. 70
20. Tripod with horizontal copy arm.
    Illustration © Anne Leaver, CC BY 4.0. 71
21. EAP698, Digitising Cham manuscripts in Vietnam.
    Photo © Hao Phan, CC BY 4.0. 72
22. Finding a solution when your copy stand breaks: EAP569,
    Using a weaving loom to digitise Nzema cultural material
    from Ghana. Photo © Samuel Nobah, CC BY 4.0. 73

List of figures 3

23. EAP454, Relying on basic desk lamps as the field workers move around the remote area of Mizoram, India.
    Photo © Kyle Jackson, CC BY 4.0.   75

24. EAP764, Blocking out sunlight when digitising material from Bandiagara, Mali.
    Photo © Fabrizio Magnani, CC BY 4.0.   76

25. Drawn illustration showing the flashgun/umbrella set-up angled at 45 degrees to the copy surface.
    Illustration © Anne Leaver, CC BY 4.0.   77

26. Equipment set-up for digitising glass plate negatives using a copy stand and a light box.
    Illustration © Anne Leaver, CC BY 4.0.   79

27. EAP563, Scanning photographs from the Hume family collection, Argentina.
    Photo © Silvana Lucia Piga, CC BY 4.0.   88

28. EAP086, A temporary scanning set-up while digitising photographs in a monastery in Laos.
    Photo © Martin Jürgens, CC BY 4.0.   91

29. Preventing light appearing in an image.
    Photos © Elizabeth Hunter, CC BY 4.0.   105

30. Building up foam beneath a bound book with a tight spine.
    Photos © Elizabeth Hunter, CC BY 4.0.   109

31. Step-by-step method for opening and supporting a folded map that is included within a bound book.
    Photos © Elizabeth Hunter, CC BY 4.0.   111

32. Diagram showing the correct brushing direction for a bound volume. Illustration © Anne Leaver, CC BY 4.0.   115

33. Book diagram and book binding terminology.
    Illustrations © Anne Leaver, CC BY 4.0.   118

34. EAP703, Digitising notary books in Bahia, Brazil.
    Photo © João Reis, CC BY 4.0.   122

35. Example document tracking form.
    Photo © Andrew Pearson, CC BY 4.0.   124

36. Example digitisation tracking form.
    Illustration © Andrew Pearson, CC BY 4.0.   124

37. A field-based system for backup.
    Illustration © Andrew Pearson, CC BY 4.0.   135

38. EAP256, Listing taking place alongside photography in
    Tamale, Ghana. Photo © Ismail Montana, CC BY 4.0.   137

39. EAP526, Theory meets practical realities in Ethiopia.
    Photo © Michael Gervers, CC BY 4.0.   139

40. EAP688, Fragile subjects.
    Photo © Kenneth Morgan, CC BY 4.0.   140

41. EAP061, A custom-made copy stand, Indonesia.
    Photo © Amiq Ahyad, CC BY 4.0.   145

42. EAP698, On the road in Vietnam.
    Photo © Hao Phan, CC BY 4.0.   146

43. EAP334, Digital preservation of Wolof Ajami manuscripts
    of Senegal. Photo © Fallou Ngom, CC BY 4.0.   155

44. EAP627, Staff training in Paraíba, Brazil.
    Photo © Courtney Campbell, CC BY 4.0.   161

45. EAP524, Historic doodles.
    Photo © Andrew Pearson, CC BY 4.0.   163

46. EAP051, BBC World Service radio programme on the
    importance of Bamum manuscripts, Cameroon.
    Photo © Konrad Tuchscherer, CC BY 4.0.   167

47. EAP596, Newspaper cuttings photographed as part of the
    Anguilla EAP's 'Digitisation Day'.
    Photo © Andrew Pearson, CC BY 4.0.   169

48. EAP177, Delivering the goods: hard drives ready for
    postage from Laos. Photo © Martin Jürgens, CC BY 4.0.   172

List of tables

1. Example quantifications, estimated by page counting and shelf length — 28
2. Sample data and labour quantification — 33
3. EAP standards for digital material — 97
4. Summary of backup rules — 133

Contributors

Jody Butterworth attended the International School of Geneva with students from 80 different countries and it is very probably this happy experience that has shaped her interests. She has spent seven years living and working across Asia and whilst in Mongolia she became inspired to pursue a career in cultural heritage. Jody became EAP Curator in 2012 and she considers it an incredibly rewarding job.

Adam Farquhar directs the Endangered Archives Programme. He is also Head of Digital Scholarship at the British Library, where he and his team focus on establishing services for researchers that take full advantage of the possibilities presented by digital collections and data across all formats and subjects. Adam has led several major research efforts and established the digital preservation and data programmes at the British Library. He was a founding member of the International Image Interoperability (IIIF) Consortium executive committee; founding President of DataCite; and founding President of the Open Preservation Foundation. He has been responsible for the Library's maps, newspaper, photographic, audio and moving image collections. Before joining the Library, he was the knowledge management architect for Schlumberger and research scientist at the Stanford University Knowledge Systems Laboratory.

Elizabeth Hunter joined the British Library Photographic Studio in 1988, which at the time was based at the British Museum and involved studio and location photography as well as black-and-white film processing. When the British Library moved to its current location in 1998, Elizabeth used the Library's first DSLR camera to photograph the Queen officially open the new building. Elizabeth keeps up to date with the latest developments and is currently working on 360VR and 3D photography.

Flavio Marzo was born in Susa near Turin in Italy. He now lives in London where he has been working for the British Library since 2005 and became an ICON accredited conservator in 2012. He previously worked in prominent institutions such as the Vatican Library and the libraries of The Queen's and Magdalen Colleges in Oxford, and also as private conservator/restorer in the Benedictine Monastery of Novalesa in Italy. He has also been involved in several conservation projects in Italy, Greece and Egypt as conservator, consultant and teacher. In 2012, Flavio was appointed Conservation Studio Manager for the Qatar Digitisation Project within the British Library/Qatar Foundation partnership. He is also the author of a number of articles published in conservation journals.

Andrew Pearson is a Senior Heritage Consultant with AECOM. He also holds Research Associate status at Brunel University. His doctoral and early-career research focused on Roman Britain, while his current research addresses the historical archaeology of the Atlantic slave trade, with particular reference to the island of St Helena and the Anglophone Caribbean. His projects for the Endangered Archives Programme comprise EAP524 (St Helena), EAP596 (Anguilla), EAP688 and EAP1013 (both St Vincent) and EAP794 (Nevis).

Patrick Sutherland is an independent photographer and former Professor of Documentary Photography at the University of the Arts London. For over two decades Patrick has been documenting the culturally Tibetan communities of the Spiti Valley in North India. The project has led to numerous exhibitions and two books: *Spiti* and *Disciples of a Crazy Saint*. The latter concerns the Buchen, travelling lay religious theatre performers, exorcists, musicians and healers unique to Spiti, whose material culture is the focus of Sutherland's two Endangered Archive Programme grants, EAP548 and EAP749.

Foreword

Adam Farquhar

From the blistering heat to the freezing cold. From desert sand to salty ocean air. From high mountains to humid jungles. From the open air under direct sun to cramped and shadowy huts. The project teams that we have supported under the Endangered Archives Programme (EAP) have worked in all of these environments and more as they digitise the world's at-risk documentary heritage, preserve it, and make it available for research.

As Director of the EAP, I have been inspired by these project teams. The more I learned about their day-to-day experiences and the different challenges they faced compared to the digitisation projects we manage in London, the more I realised how useful it would be to compile their knowledge and experience in book form. To accomplish this, we assembled an excellent team with in-depth experience of field digitisation projects, studio digitisation, and material handling. Working together, they have created this book. While we have written it with Endangered Archives projects in mind, it has much broader applicability.

We hope that this book will help anyone who takes part in field digitisation projects. It provides clear practical advice that should help you if you are trying to plan, manage and deliver such a project, with topics ranging from the organisation and listing of contents, the digitisation of delicate materials, and the use of metadata to describe the results accurately.

The EAP is funded by Arcadia, a charitable fund of Lisbet Rausing and Peter Baldwin, which supports the preservation of cultural heritage and promotes open access. It is through the generosity of Arcadia that we have been able to create this volume and make it available to all on an open access basis.

We have created and published this book together with Open Book Publishers to ensure that neither cost nor access would be a barrier to a potential reader anywhere in the world. In addition to the book itself – which can be a handy reference in the field and does not require a reliable electrical supply to read – we have also provided a set of online appendices that will be updated as equipment or recommendations change. We also welcome feedback from readers so that future editions reflect the best available practices.

We hope that this volume helps you and many others to digitise and preserve the world's endangered documentary heritage – including the piece of it that is important to you, your family, and your community.

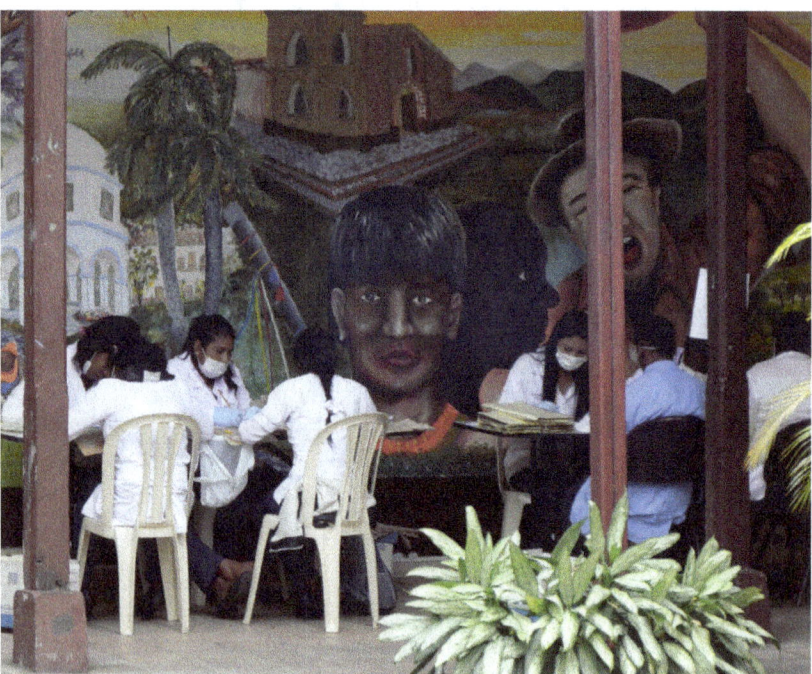

Figure 1. EAP650, Archiving Afro-Colombian history in Caloto Viejo, Colombia. Photo © Thomas Desch Obi, CC BY 4.0.

Acknowledgements

The Endangered Archives Programme staff would like to thank everyone who has contributed to this publication and, in particular, Anthea Case and Maja Kominko at Arcadia for backing the initial idea. We are indebted to Matt Faber, who was extremely kind in sharing his knowledge on scanning equipment, to Anne Leaver who worked conscientiously on the illustrations, to Alastair Horne who was so meticulous when proofreading the final draft, and to Hugh Pearson for his contribution to the text and drawings in Digital Appendix 1. Meanwhile, the process notes set out in Digital Appendix 2 draw heavily on the work undertaken by Ben Jeffs during the EAP project on Anguilla. Thanks also go to the British Library managers Karl Harris and Sarah-Jane Hamlyn, who supported Elizabeth Hunter and Flavio Marzo's involvement with the book. We would also like to express our gratitude to the external reviewers: Andreas Nef, David Small and Wayne Torborg, whose experience and comments have helped us enormously. We also are very grateful to Open Book Publishers, who have been approachable, helpful and patient as the book progressed.

To our minds, what has made this publication so special are the very honest experiences shared and the wonderful photographs of projects being carried out in the field. EAP would like to thank all of those who contributed: Amiq Ahyad; Hans Berger; Abhijit Bhattacharya; Courtney Campbell; Ananya Chakravarti; Yasmine Chemali; Graeme Counsel; Birgit Embaló; Michael Gervers; Poppy Gogoi; Zoé Headley; Kyle Jackson; Ben Jeffs; Martin Jürgens; Alexander Keese; David LaFevor; Joseph Lalzarliana; Fabrizio Magnani; Ismail Montana; Stephen Morey;

Kenneth Morgan; Appasamy Murugaiyan; N. Murugesan; Fallou Ngom; Samuel Nobah; Thomas Desch Obi; Silvana Lucia Piga; Hao Phan; Karma Phuntsho; Tim Procter; João Reis; Nigel Sadler; Sophie Sarin; David Small; Fakhriati Thahir; Joel Thaulo; Konrad Tuchscherer; Fernando Valle; Jian Xu; Hastings Zidana; and all of those who are depicted in the photographs but have not been named, without whom EAP would not be such a success.

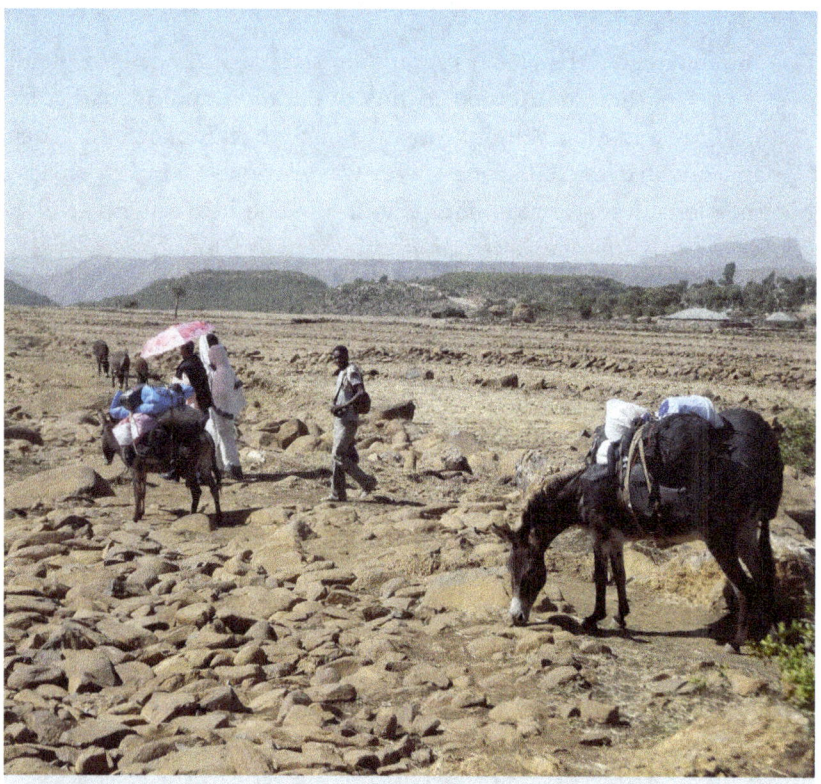

Figure 2. EAP704, En route to Marawe Krestos, Ethiopia.
Photo © Michael Gervers, CC BY 4.0.

A note on the text boxes

As a part of this project, a number of past and present EAP grant holders were contacted and asked to provide a narrative about their experiences. Geographically, they span Africa, Asia, Central and South America, and the Caribbean, and embrace a wide variety of political and social circumstances. Collectively, they have been an invaluable resource during the writing of this book, offering general advice and a flavour of project experiences.

It was not possible to reproduce these responses in full and, in certain cases, it would have been inappropriate to do so. This was particularly the case for responses dealing with projects that are either still active or only recently finished, and those that talk candidly about local circumstances. Where possible, the selected quotations are attributed to their author and project, but a number have been anonymised and sometimes slightly rewritten, so as to maintain confidentiality.

Brands and manufacturers

Within this book, reference is made to certain equipment manufacturers and software brands. This has been necessary because otherwise, at points in the book, an adequate discussion would not have been possible. The issue is even more apparent within the digital appendices, which could not have been compiled without specific references to particular brands, models and software.

In some cases, above all for cameras, there is an accepted 'industry standard'. In these cases we do make specific recommendations about what should be purchased for an EAP project (see Digital Appendix 4). However, elsewhere we discuss items for which there are several viable options. This is particularly true when it comes to software. In these instances no recommendation should be implied, even where a product is specifically mentioned.

Digital resources

This book is accompanied by a series of digital appendices. These provide detailed information about certain aspects of a digitisation project, as follows:

Digital Appendix 1. Practical Methods for Digitisation

Digital Appendix 2. Using Electronic Flash

Digital Appendix 3. Digitisation Process Notes

Digital Appendix 4. Costed Equipment List

These resources may be found at https://doi.org/10.11647/OBP.0138.11

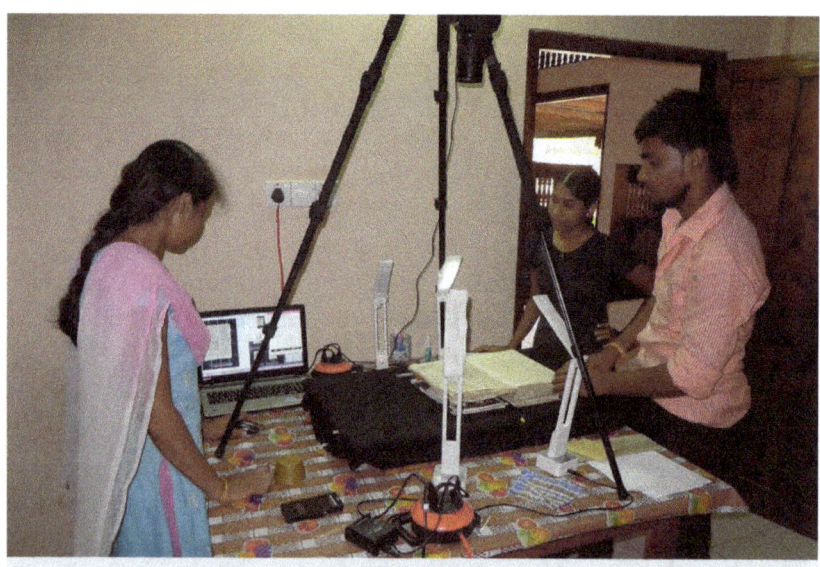

Figure 3. EAP700, Preserving the manuscripts of the Jaffna Bishop's House, Sri Lanka. Photo © Appasamy Murugaiyan, CC BY 4.0.

Introduction

Jody Butterworth

The Endangered Archives Programme (EAP) was set up in 2004 with an initial grant of £10 million from Arcadia and is administered by the British Library. The purpose of the programme is to contribute to the preservation of documentary heritage, which is at risk of neglect, physical deterioration or destruction in areas of the world where resources are more limited, primarily within Africa, Asia, Latin America and parts of Europe. This is achieved by the annual award of grants that enable applicants to locate relevant endangered archival collections, to arrange their transfer to a suitable local archival home where appropriate, to create digital copies of the material and to deposit these with local institutions and the British Library. To date, it has funded over 300 projects in more than 90 countries whose variety and scope has been astounding. As a result, the programme currently has over 6 million images online.

After the excitement of the tenth anniversary celebrations began to die down, the Endangered Archives team realised that there was a wealth of knowledge and experience gained from all the projects across the world, and that this information should be collated to provide advice for future projects that would probably encounter very similar issues. Many grant holders had succeeded (sometimes against all odds) in extremely inaccessible and challenging locations and the EAP team felt it was important to share this unique and valuable knowledge. This book is the result. Its aim is to try to prevent anyone from having to learn from scratch in comparable scenarios. The intention is to boost the confidence of anyone about to embark on a digitisation project (perhaps for the first time) and who may not have the luxury of having a colleague nearby whose expertise they can call upon. We hope that by giving clear guidance about the processes involved and the standards that EAP expects, the quality of material produced by any project will be of a uniformly high standard.

Of course, no two projects are alike and this book cannot be prescriptive in the advice that it gives. The most important thing we have learnt from reading the final reports from the many project holders is the need to be flexible and resourceful. The types of grants awarded have been so varied that we cannot adopt a 'one size fits all' attitude. Some projects are based in one location and have the luxury of a dedicated space within an institution to digitise, while others are peripatetic, searching for material held in private family collections. Some projects have had regular and reliable electricity supplies, whilst others have not. EAP has an extremely broad view of the term 'archive' and this will also impact on how to digitise — a tightly bound manuscript, a glass plate negative, a map or a brittle publication will all need different approaches. The recommendations in these pages have all been tried and tested. Part of the book has been written by previous grant holders, who have experienced what an EAP project entails for themselves, and the remainder has been written by British Library staff, so the standards we require from EAP projects will not differ from those that we set ourselves.

Digitisation is complex and although there are many resources available, there is nothing that quite targets the specialist needs of any current or prospective EAP applicant. A potential EAP grant holder needs to become an expert in so many disciplines: they are required to be competent at project management; be able to accurately assess the amount of material they anticipate digitising in a certain timeframe; and they are expected to foresee what measures they should have in place if they are working in an area with unpredictable resources. In addition, any grant holder is also expected to produce images to a professional standard and to understand the equipment suitable for digitisation projects — not only camera models and lenses, but also the specialist knowledge of preferred models that have more robust sealants for dusty or humid environments. Grant holders will need technical knowledge about image capture, to know the correct file formats for archival purposes, and have an understanding of digital preservation — basically, everything that means an image will comply with British Library standards. Finally, there are the truly unique concerns for some projects, such as how conventional laptop and external hard drives are vulnerable to the effects of high altitude.

Many of the projects do not have the luxury of state-of-the-art facilities. They are projects on the move, often photographing rare and precious manuscripts in people's homes or at various institutions where compromises may have to be made. For example, some projects have found it necessary to digitise outside in natural daylight because there has been no electricity supply.

We hope this book covers all of the essential skills needed for an EAP grant. Chapter 1 considers project planning and management. This is, of course, a discipline in its own right, and so the chapter is necessarily limited to the basic essentials; those wishing to learn about project management as a whole will probably need to consult other resources. The purpose here is to outline some of the key issues specific to a digitisation project in the field. This begins at the planning stage, before funding has even been obtained, and then moves on to the phase when the project is up and running. Chapter 2 offers a comprehensive guide to the type of equipment you will need if you choose either a digital SLR camera or a scanner. On the whole, camera set-ups are the most suitable for EAP projects, and the chapter therefore concentrates on the workings of a camera, and on how to set up the equipment for optimum capture. Scanning technologies and capture methods are addressed more briefly. Chapter 3 focusses on the standards required for digitisation, including a section comprising illustrative images that follow our guidelines and those that do not. Although EAP does not fund conservation as part of its awards, it is important to consider preservation issues when undertaking a digitisation project and this is discussed in Chapter 4. Chapter 5 gives a step-by-step process for the workflow to ensure that each stage is carried out correctly, while Chapter 6 deals with practicalities and guidance when in the field, with many examples from previous grant holders.

These chapters are also accompanied by a series of digital appendices.[1] These provide further detailed guidance about certain aspects. Appendix 1 offers a pair of practical methods for digitisation in

---

1   These resources may be found at https://doi.org/10.11647/OBP.0138.11

the field, one using a portable book cradle ideal for small fragile bound manuscripts, the other using a custom built 'slide table' more suitable for studio settings; the methods of making both the cradle and slide table are also included. Appendix 2 provides detailed advice on how to set up electronic flash in your digitisation studio. Appendix 3 contains step-by-step process notes for digitising with a standard camera and software suite. Finally, Appendix 4 gives a costed list of equipment for a digitisation project.

If you are reading this book because you have just been awarded an EAP grant, then we hope you find it useful. If you have picked it up because you are toying with the idea of applying, then we hope that by the time you have reached the end of the book, you feel that you can apply — and we look forward to reading your application. On a personal note, as EAP Curator, it has been an extremely humbling experience to read the final reports of numerous grant holders. From the comfort of my desk at St Pancras, I have been transported all around the world and have heard about the tireless efforts and resourceful solutions that the teams have used to ensure the successful outcomes of their projects. Without their passion and enthusiasm, the Endangered Archives Programme would not be the success that I believe it is, and I would like to take this opportunity to thank everyone who has been involved with an EAP project. It is due to their dedication that the Programme has been able to make completely unique and previously unknown material available for scholarship.

1. Planning the project

Andrew Pearson

Project design

While perhaps not the most glamorous aspects of a project, its scope, budget and practical planning are critical. All these matters need to be considered at the very outset and the following sections consider the ways that, through detailed advance planning, it is possible to create the circumstances for a successful project.

- ☐ Establish the scope of the project. While it is important to have a clear sense of the overall objectives, it is also critical that there be a precise understanding of the detail. In other words, it is not enough to aspire to digitise a particular collection: you must also be able to quantify the size of the task.

- ☐ Do your research. Try to learn as much as possible about the collection you wish to digitise, as well as the local circumstances in which you will be working. Although there will doubtless be unknown factors and undecided detail, the better informed you are, the more likely it is that your approach will be appropriate to the task.

- ☐ Build partnerships in the host country. Having local links will be invaluable throughout the project, providing — amongst other things — a source of knowledge, a conduit for communication, and immediate help when practical problems emerge. Local interest in what you are doing will also make the whole experience more enjoyable and rewarding.

- Manage your own and others' **expectations**. Be realistic about what you think you can achieve within the scope and budget of your project. In the first instance, this is necessary to convince grant-awarding bodies that yours is a viable project: applications that are over-ambitious or under-costed may be perceived as naïve and are likely to be rejected. In the mid-term, it is you who will be responsible for delivering the project on time and within budget. Avoid setting yourself a stressful, unachievable task. Finally, at the close of the project, it is important that you deliver what is promised. The funding body has awarded money on the basis of your scope and will expect you to meet it. In short, do not promise what you cannot achieve. It is better to offer less but deliver more, rather than the other way around.

- Think also about **outcomes**. Local partners may have their own expectations of what you will do for them. Meeting these expectations is critical, not only for your own professional standards, but in case future funding is going to be sought or long-term local partnerships developed.

- There are also specific issues to be thought through when considering the **project's conclusion**. For example, who will have access to the data? Ideally, how will you ensure it is widely accessible, and sufficiently well-publicised for people to know it exists? What hardware might be needed in order for access to be possible or practical? How many hard drives will you be distributing locally, and to which institutions? Do you need an agreement to migrate data to a local government server?

- Seek **advice**. While this book provides guidance, it can be neither comprehensive nor project-specific. There is no substitute for conversations with people who have undertaken projects of a similar scope, and with those either living in, or with experience of, the place where you will work.

☐ Obtain **permission**. This is absolutely critical, as all efforts will be wasted if agreement is not obtained locally for permission to access the materials, digitise them and disseminate the product. Ensure that this permission is formally set down, in a letter or email, by a person with the authority to give it. Make sure that person fully understands what they are agreeing, to avoid the risk of permission being rescinded at a later stage. (For further discussion of permissions and open access see page 150.)

Endangered Archives Programme grants

The Endangered Archives Programme offers two types of grant: a Pilot project or a Major award. The first type allows for a preliminary investigation or audit of archival collections on a particular subject, in a discrete region, or in a specific format. Pilot projects are also an opportunity to determine the feasibility of digitisation, and in many cases involve the trialling of photography or scanning. They are also a means of judging the technical competence of the grant holder, the likelihood of them succeeding with a full-scale project, and whether external specialists might need to be added to the team.

Some archival collections are sufficiently small to be captured within a Pilot project. Major grants are generally larger and the projects more protracted. Depending on circumstances, some follow immediately from the pilot phase, while others have resumed after an interval of several years.

Grant awards for both Pilot and Major projects are made annually and are assessed by an International Advisory Panel. The Panel often likes to see initial applications for a Pilot project before progressing to a Major grant.

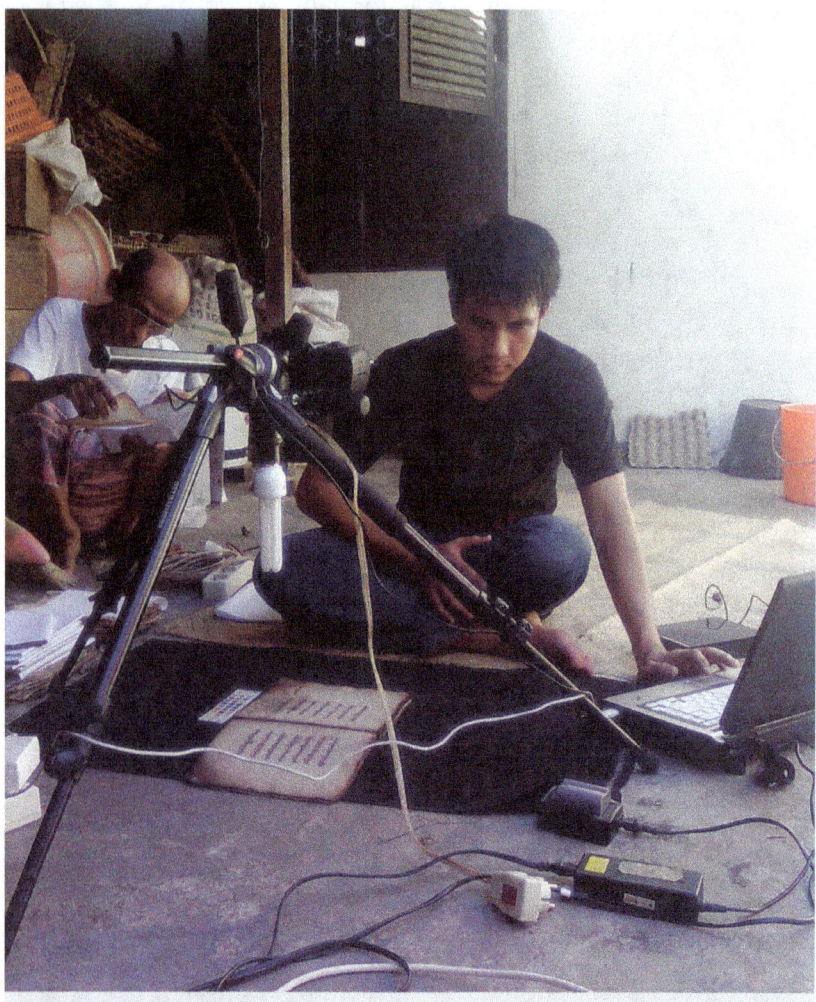

Figure 4. EAP329, A peripatetic project digitising Acehnese manuscripts in rudimentary circumstances, Indonesia.
Photo © Fakhriati Thahir, CC BY 4.0.

Once I had identified a funding agency, I requested the support of my advisor to co-direct the projects with me and sought the advice of others who had carried out digitisation projects. By consulting sample grant applications, I was able to create a realistic list of equipment [...] Writing the final grant application cannot be done at the last minute or overnight. It is important to start planning these projects about a year before you plan to begin digitisation.

Courtney Campbell, EAP627 and EAP853, Brazil

I had no experience of digitising records, but I did know the island and its historical resources. Either get some training in digitisation to archival standard, or team up with an experienced person from the start.

David Small, EAP093 and EAP794, Nevis

I would recommend that anyone intending to undertake an EAP project reads other final reports, especially in the region of the world they are working, and talk with former grant recipients. This saved me a lot of time and meant a successful process for digitisation that had worked in Anguilla could be modified to work in Montserrat.

Nigel Sadler, EAP769, Montserrat

Our formal point of liaison was with the national government, but when trying to set up the project its officials were often woefully slow to communicate. Fortunately, we were also in contact with the director of the heritage society who, when progress came to a halt, would visit the relevant officials and cajole them into taking action!

> We also had the challenge of photographing large leaves of books that did not fit into a scanner, and which would not fit into the image frame of the camera, even at the tallest setting of the copy stand (which was the biggest available to buy). Instead, we devised a way of putting the texts on a wooden board, placed parallel to the camera on a tripod.
>
> *Karma Phuntsho, EAP039, Bhutan*

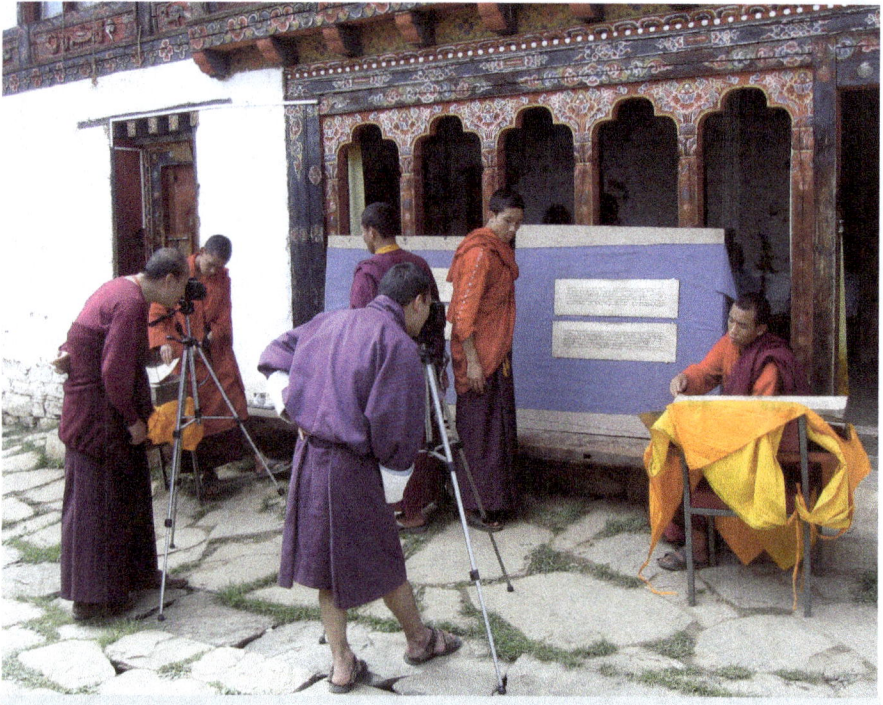

Figure 5. EAP039, Photographing Buddhist manuscripts in Bhutan.
These manuscripts were too large to be photographed beneath a tripod or camera stand, so instead were attached to a board, allowing them to be photographed from a greater distance. (N.B. The securing pins were immediately above and below the manuscripts, rather than pierced through them.) Photo © Karma Phuntsho, CC BY 4.0.

Calculating the budget

Project budgets can broadly be divided into two basic headings: salaries, and non-salary costs. The first of these comprises the wages of those being paid directly by the project, as well as replacement costs for staff who are being seconded to the project. Non-salary costs incorporate all other elements of the budget, from purchases of equipment and supplies to travel, accommodation, subsistence and items such as freight shipping, and personal and equipment insurance.

Equipment specifications are discussed in the following section, while most other non-salary costs will be specific to an individual project. This section therefore focuses on how the human inputs of a digitisation exercise can be quantified. In most mid- to larger-sized projects that address significant volumes of material, staff costs will be the dominant part of the budget.

Choosing your equipment

Appropriate equipment for digitisation is discussed separately within this book. However, every project is different and there is no 'one size fits all' solution. When specifying equipment, therefore, consider the following:

- **Subject**. What means of digitisation is most appropriate to your documents? Should you be purchasing a camera, scanner, or a combination of these items?
- **Location**. Where will the digitisation take place? Will you be working in multiple places, requiring you to have a compact, portable set of equipment? Alternatively, will you be based in a single location where you could set up a basic studio? In the latter case, you could consider less portable items, such as a copy stand and studio lamps, as well as desktop computers and a larger monitor, instead of a laptop.
- **Compatibility**. Do your purchases need to integrate with, or complement, existing equipment? For example, does your local partner already own a particular brand of camera and lenses?

Simple issues also require thought: for example, whether the plugs on your electrical leads are compatible with the local supply. If you are working with a local government, it is also possible that its IT department will only maintain or support computers from certain manufacturers.

- **Legacy**. The end-use of your equipment is also a factor if it is to be donated locally at the end of the project. (N.B. This is a stipulation of all EAP grants.) Consider what would be most useful: for example, would the library or archive benefit from owning a copy stand? Equally, consider if certain items might simply be consigned to a cupboard and never used. Taking the same example, an expensive tripod — though useful to your project — is probably not an appropriate item for long-term public use in a reading room. The question of compatibility is also relevant.

As the preceding points illustrate, subject, location and various other factors will influence the choice of equipment for a digitisation project. However, for any project there are absolute essentials, while for a less minimalistic project there are additional items that can potentially improve the product, speed up productivity, or both.

> Consider local travel and the time it takes — will getting from your accommodation to the institution eat into the working day? Is it feasible to use local public transport or will you need to arrange cars and drivers?
>
> If running an itinerant project, plan your travel itinerary carefully with a view to efficiency. Make sure that you do not have to retrace your steps. Equally, factor in some flexibility to your time and budget, in case your plans have to change.

Quantifying the collection

The time and labour required to undertake a project will principally depend on the size of the collection and the rate at which material of this type can be digitised. The more precisely these factors can be quantified, the more confidence can be placed in the resultant cost estimates and timescale.

There are various ways that the size of a collection may be quantified, depending on the extent (if any) of access to the collection during the planning stage.[1]

- **Individual page count.** This enables the most precise quantification but is only feasible for relatively small collections, or for document groups where the pages of each volume are numbered. It is clearly not practical to count the unnumbered pages of every book in a large collection.
- **Sample page count/number of volumes.** This is a reduced page-counting exercise, in which a sample of representative material is quantified, and the result extrapolated to the collection as a whole (i.e. number of pages per 'average' volume, multiplied by the total number of volumes).
- **Sample page count/shelf width.** In this method, page counts are made for a sample of the collection — again, these being representative examples of the whole. The width of each volume is also measured, allowing for a calculation of pages per millimetre. Total shelf length is then measured. The two figures can then be multiplied to estimate the total number of pages.

For the two latter methods, it is self-evident that the larger the sample, the greater the precision of the overall estimate. Both produce only approximate results and, as Table 1 shows, applying the two methods to the same collection produces different figures — in this case varying by 5%. The higher figure needs to be taken forward for the calculation of time inputs and data storage requirements.

---

[1] A more detailed discussion of collection preparation and survey is given by Anna Bülow and Jess Ahmon, in *Preparing Collections for Digitisation* (London: Facet Publishing in association with the UK National Archives, 2011).

Of course, if you have very little information about a collection, your 'estimate' will be little more than a guess. This is an understandable scenario, given that you may be dealing with a collection to which you do not yet have access, or are contemplating a project where the material is scattered across numerous locations — perhaps held by multiple private individuals. In such instances, the only recourse is to estimate the time requirements very conservatively — or, in fact, consider whether the first stage of your project is simply dedicated to reconnaissance and quantification.

In quantifying the collection, it also becomes possible to reach precise figures for the amount of data that will be generated. This, in turn, informs you about the volume of digital storage that will be needed — once again feeding back into your equipment list and budget calculations. Table 2 (see p. 33), based on a real-world example, shows both of these steps. In this instance, the size of the collection was well understood, a pilot project having allowed for most of the books to be individually page-counted.

Table 1. Example quantifications, estimated by page counting and shelf length. Example taken from EAP524 St Helena. Sample method: the volumes were taken from all shelves. The choice of volumes from a given shelf was essentially random, though if different types of binding or styles of book were present an attempt was made to take a representative sample.

Sample size

Number of volumes page-counted = 104

Total number of volumes in the collection = 1007

Percentage of volumes page-counted = 10.3%

Estimate by page count per volume

Average number of pages per volume = 305 (based on 104 volumes, comprising a total of 31688 pages)

Total number of pages = 305 pages x 1007 volumes = **307,135 pages**

Estimate by page count per mm

Average thickness per volume = 47mm (based on 104 volumes, occupying 4847mm of shelf width)

Average no. pages per mm = 6.54 (based on 31688 pages occupying 4847mm of shelf width)

Total shelf width = 44,800mm

Total number of pages = 44,800mm of shelf x 6.54 pages/mm = **292,992 pages**

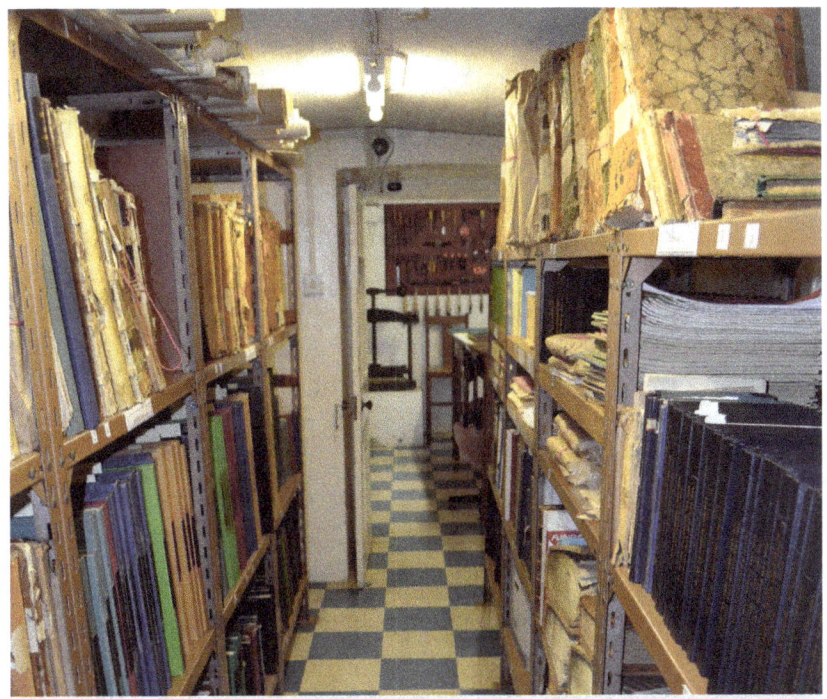

Figure 6. EAP524, The St Helena Government Archives, Jamestown. EAP524 centred on a survey of this collection, including the quantification exercise shown in Table 1. Photo © Andrew Pearson, CC BY 4.0.

It would have been helpful to know in advance just how much data the project would produce. With hindsight we would have put more money into the budget for portable hard drives if we had realised the size of the data required, and for the time required to convert the RAW files to TIFF.

Stephen Morey and Poppy Gogoi, EAP373, Assam

Factor in enough time for cataloguing the collection [i.e. Listing], because it might be very difficult and time-consuming to decide the names and contents, especially when those materials are in an endangered language.

Jian Xu, EAP012, EAP081, EAP143, EAP217, EAP460 and EAP550, China

Timescale and labour requirements

Having established the size of the task, the second step is to calculate the rate of digitisation. If you do not have prior experience of digitisation, seek the advice of others — ideally those who have worked with similar materials. Alternatively, if you have the luxury of a two-stage project, the initial phase can be used to trial the equipment and establish a realistic work rate, using the actual collection.

When making an estimate, it is useful to break the calculation down into small increments. In other words, start by thinking about how long it will take to lay out and photograph a single page, and then factor up from there. This is likely to be more realistic than basing your estimate on broader and possibly rather vague assumptions: for example, 'it should be possible to digitise one volume per day'.

Finally, before arriving at your definitive estimate for time inputs, consider how theory will meet practice in the real world. For example:

- **Slow beginnings.** At the outset of a project, despite your own enthusiasm, events may (and probably will) progress slowly. It takes time to get set up, as you hold meetings with the relevant people in authority, finalise your permissions for access and copying, and cross the myriad minor hurdles which inevitably attend a new enterprise. It is not unusual to lose days or even a few weeks at the outset, particularly if you are working in a place with a complex local bureaucracy. Factor this extra time into your budget.

- **Non-productive time** will persist throughout the project. Remember that the slick, efficient workflow you envisage at the planning stage is unlikely to manifest itself in the real world. Consider, for example, how much time will be needed to move documents from their place of storage to where they will be digitised and back again. Alternatively, you may have to travel between venues to carry out on-site digitisation. Other crucial activities also take time, such as the backing up of data. Productivity also has the potential to fall because of IT problems or equipment failure.

- **Document sizes and condition.** The physical size and condition of a document may well influence the time it will take to lay out and digitise. Large format items may be more difficult to lay out, while the necessary delicate handling of damaged or brittle materials will be slower than for robust items in good condition.

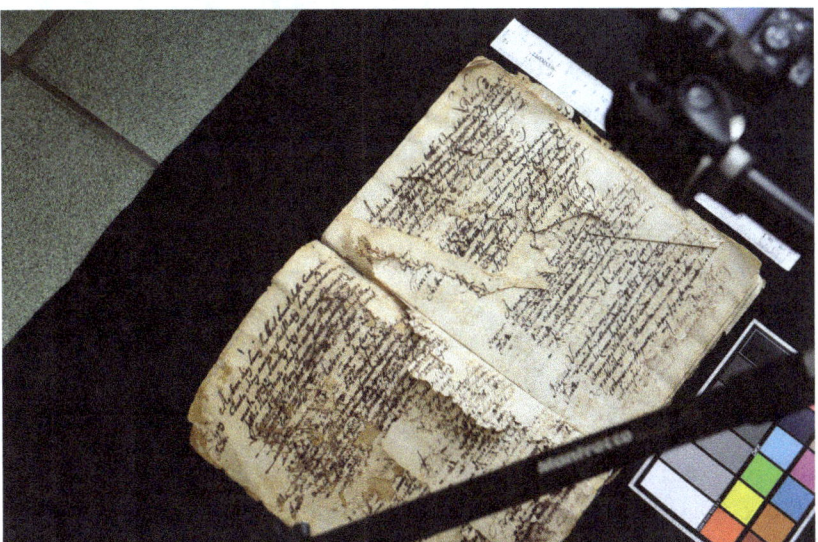

Figure 7. EAP627, A fragile manuscript from Paraíba, Brazil.
Consider how the physical condition of your documents might affect the speed of your digitisation. Photo © Courtney Campbell, CC BY 4.0.

- **Productivity.** Your own work rate may not be an accurate reflection of your staff work rate. During project planning you may have trialled the digitisation process yourself, or simply have a sense of how quickly it should proceed. Be cautious, however. While you might keep up a certain pace for a few days or weeks, ask whether this is sustainable for a staff member over the long term. Additionally, if you are delivering a project in an area with different cultural expectations, you may find that attitudes to work may be more relaxed than your own — perhaps markedly so.

- **Size of workforce.** Two staff members may be better than one... but not necessarily as productive. Digitisation is a precise, demanding, but repetitive exercise. A single staff member, working in isolation over a long period, has the potential to become disillusioned and demotivated. Having two or more staff tends to head off this problem, and also has the benefit that they can cross-check each other's work. Arguably, this leads to a higher-quality product. On the other hand, two members of staff, working side-by-side with a single camera, will not be digitising at twice the rate of a single person. Consider this possibility in your 'person-day' calculations.

- **Don't underestimate your own inputs.** As project manager, the amount of time you will need at the beginning of a project is deceptively large, with tasks ranging from local liaison to travel bookings and the ordering, testing and shipping of equipment. The same is true of the tasks at the end, such as report-writing and the archiving of data. In between, keeping the project running smoothly can often consume much more time than you ever expected, particularly if problems arise that require you to solve them.

The final part of Table 2 shows how the figures for page count and work rate combine to produce an estimate of the total number of person-days for the entire project. The calculations produce an exact figure but, as discussed above, this has to be treated as an unrealistic minimum. The last rows of the table therefore depart from the calculations to offer a more subjective, but ultimately more realistic, 'real-world' figure. In this case, there was good reason to downgrade the work rate very considerably. The documents in question were held in a different building to the place where digitisation was carried out, a situation that added considerable time to proceedings. Moreover, the local staff were also delegated the tasks of exporting their original RAW images to TIFF format, as well as being responsible for data backup and cataloguing. For all of these reasons, their real-world progress would necessarily be much slower than the theoretical rate — in this case roughly half. And, although not shown on the table, additional time was added to the budget because two staff members were working with a single camera set-up: as noted in the bullet-points above, this creates a good work environment but, in terms of person-days, one that is less productive in absolute terms.

Finally, be philosophical! Accept that difficulties and delays will be an integral part of your project. Be patient, addressing problems in as relaxed a way as you can. Seek to control the controllables, but do not become agitated about matters that you cannot influence.

Table 2. Sample data and labour quantification.
Original quantification submitted in the grant application for EAP794 Nevis. In the event, the project proceeded with two staff members. The scope was slightly reduced, as one group of documents was not accessible for digitisation, with the project achieved in approximately 450 person-days.

1) Original documents	
Common Deed Record Books — 52 volumes x 566 pp.	29432
Wills and Indexes of Deeds — 9 volumes x 500 pp.	4500
Land Title Register Books — 6 volumes x 395 pp.	2370
Estate plans, loose, plus 1 roll — 50 individual sheets	50
Court of Commissioners, Encumbered Estates — 2 volumes x 700 pp.	1400
Misc. Court Records — 9 volumes	3000
Court of Kings Bench/Queens Bench and Common Pleas — 42 volumes x 317 pp.	13314
Historic registers of Births Deaths and Marriages — 16 volumes and 5 boxes	5000
Miscellaneous other volumes — 34 volumes x 303 pp.	10303
Total pages to be photographed (= total images to be produced)	**69369**
2) Data Quantification	
Each RAW file (original photographs)	25mb
Each TIFF file (export format)	31mb
Total size of RAW files = 69369 x 25mb	1734225 mb
Total size of TIFF files = 69369 x 31mb	2150439 mb
Total all files (mb)	3884664 mb
Total all files (TB)	3.70 TB
3) Time quantification	
Theoretical rate:	
1 page/minute = 60 pages/hour = 420 pages/seven-hour day	
69369 images (total)/420 (no. images/day) = 165 person-days	
Real-world rate:	
Likely to be half the theoretical figure, therefore:	
330 person-days (1 x staff member)	
Equivalent to 66 five-day weeks	
or	
495 person-days (2 x staff using a single camera setup — assume 50% less productive than one person)	
Equivalent to 49.5 five day weeks per staff member	

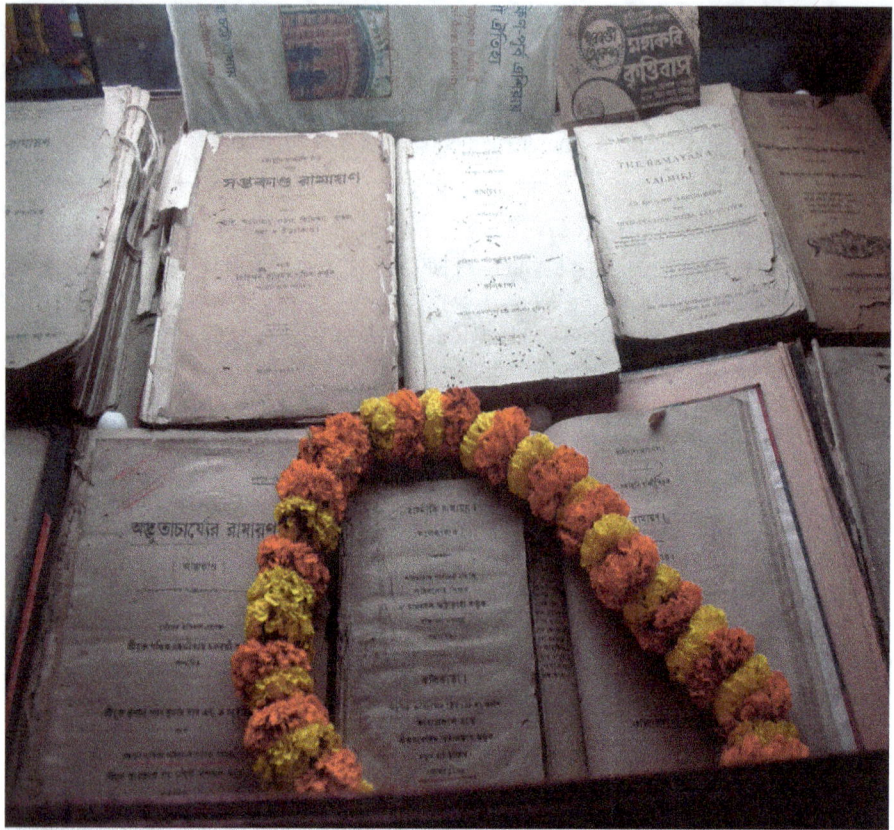

Figure 8. EAP643, Manuscripts prepared for digitisation, Bengal.
During this project, religious manuscripts required blessing before digitisation could take place. Photo © Abhijit Bhattacharya, CC BY 4.0.

I hadn't realised the extent to which the work ethics (attendance, punctuality, loyalty to the project) would differ so much from those encountered at home.

Different parts of the world have different ideas about what is correct behaviour. Local culture and attitudes need to be incorporated into the project plan. In my case, the attitude was very 'laid back' and 'local time' did not align precisely with the calendar or clock.

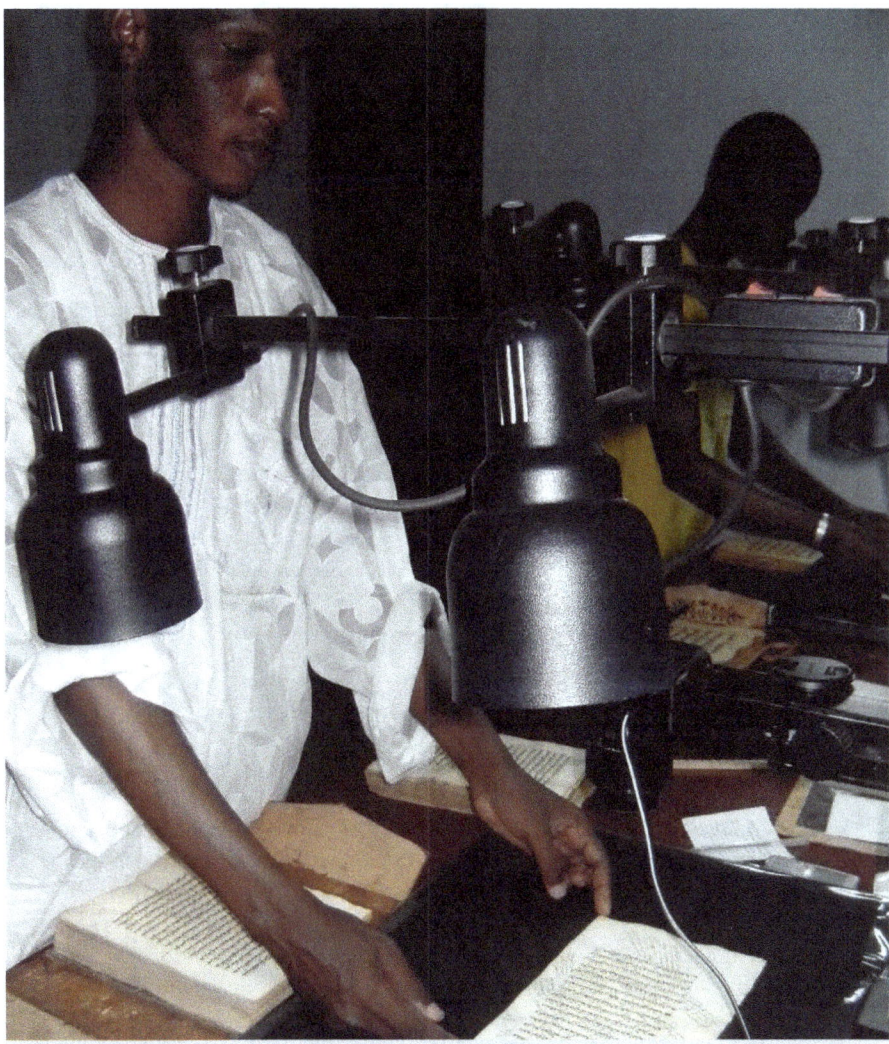

Figure 9. EAP488, An EAP team in action, Mali.
A pair of local staff members work simultaneously to digitise manuscripts from Djenné and surrounding villages. Photo © Sophie Sarin, CC BY 4.0.

Another point, specific to our research field, was the necessity to 'hand something back' in exchange for the trust and the time given to us by the document holders. It was not conceivable to 'waltz in and waltz out', but these extra activities were inevitably time-consuming.

The local research staff established a rapport with the document holders, returning upon invitation for their special family occasion (ear-boring ceremony, puberty ritual, etc.) when possible. We also organised a visit to the host institution for one of the caste headmen, which helped a great deal to establish a relationship of respect and confidence. We have systematically handed over DVD copies of the documents digitised along with photos of the team and the document holder.

Zoé Headley, EAP458, India

The working conditions in the archive were far from ideal. The archival material is exposed to dust and to the harsh environments. The archival rooms are sometimes visited by rodents but the main threat comes from the termites. At my arrival they had attacked most of the wooden shelves. The new metal shelving, purchased thanks to EAP funding, allowed us to replace the worst of the wooden shelves, while other ones have been repaired by a carpenter in the city. Restoring the shelving and making the archive accessible again were priorities needed to start working and digitising.

Fabrizio Magnani, EAP764, Mali

We mostly dealt with public institutions and had to work within them. These public spaces have their own problems and each of them is unique in nature, for example in terms of working hours: some operated from 2pm till 8pm while others had very short working hours and more than once in a day, such as 9am to 10am and again from 5pm to 7pm in the evening. The team accordingly had to adjust to all of these different timings as well as to holiday schedules.

Abhijit Bhattacharya, EAP643, Bengal

Significant amounts of time were taken in travelling across Freetown from the hotel to the museum and back, meaning working days were severely truncated. For the 2016 visit to reshoot, we moved the camera equipment and archive items to a bedroom in our hotel; this overcame the issues of heat, dust and vibration, and also allowed work to commence without a two-hour journey across Freetown!

Tim Procter, EAP626, Sierra Leone

Financial contingencies and other considerations

Finally, having arrived at estimates for labour, and also having calculated the equipment costs, it is necessary to consider the risk of overspending and the means of protecting the project against this eventuality. This is achieved through a budget contingency.

Every budget, however confident you are about its accuracy, should contain a contingency. This is necessary for reasons such as:

- **Price inflation**. The cost of budgeted items may change, whether this be equipment, flight costs or accommodation.
- **Additional purchases**. Despite meticulous planning, not all costs can be anticipated. There will always be peripheral purchases that have not been thought of.
- **Currency fluctuations**. For overseas projects, when the grant is paid in one currency but spent in another, a changing exchange rate may make locally-incurred costs and staff wages more expensive. The volatility of the currency markets at the time of writing emphasises this risk.
- **Risk management**. Broken, lost or stolen equipment may need to be replaced, wasted field visits may have to be repeated, while costs that are either unlikely or totally unexpected (damage to a hire car, for example) may be incurred. It is important that, within reason, the project is insulated from such eventualities.

In some cases, the financial contingency for a project may be allowed as a lump-sum under its own budget heading. However, this is relatively unusual, as grant-awarding bodies are generally unwilling to allocate money to non-itemised costs, or to cover 'what if' scenarios. It is more common (although less transparent) for a project contingency to be built in across the entire budget. This can be achieved by means of one, or a combination, of the following:

- Get accurate current costs for budget items, but do not use the lowest possible costs for budgeting. Remember that the actual costs at the time of purchase, which could be six to twelve months later, may be higher.

A very short drop can destroy one's equipment, especially laptops and external hard drives [...] Take one more camera and one more laptop than you think you'll need.

Michael Gervers, EAP 254, EAP340, EAP526, EAP704, Ethiopia

There was a change in government following the sudden death of the President [...] Then came 49% currency devaluation which pushed all prices of commodities above the approved budget. There was a scarcity of fuel which, when available and only on the black market, was twice the recommended pump price.

Joel Thaulo, EAP797, Malawi

At the time of submitting the detailed pilot project, the exchange rate was 1 GBP to 700 but at the time of the funds transfer, the local currency had appreciated and was trading at 645 to a Pound. However, prices of goods remained unchanged, meaning that we spent more than we had budgeted for.

Hastings Zidana, EAP714, Malawi

Mid-way through the project there was a substantial drop in the value of the Pound against the US Dollar and the other local currencies that I had to deal with. This substantially reduced the real-life value of our grant by several thousand pounds. Fortunately, economies made elsewhere in the project, combined with the built-in contingency, allowed us to achieve the project scope within the original budget.

Andrew Pearson, EAP794, Nevis

☐ Giving conservative (i.e. worst-case) costs for budget items about which you are least certain, or those which have the greatest potential to push your budget into overspend if your estimate is too low.

The overall size of the contingency needs to be determined on a project-by-project basis. Again, this is based on the perception of financial risk. How confident are you in your cost estimates? How much control will you exercise over the project, or will a great deal rest with other people, or hinge on capricious local circumstances? For whatever reason, what is the potential for matters to go wrong, with expensive consequences? In all cases a minimum of 10–15% of total budget is advisable.

10% withholding

10% of EAP grants are held back until their successful completion. This means that, if you spend up to the grant limit, you will be temporarily out of pocket. You will therefore have to consider how this temporary shortfall will be covered.

Import tax/Customs duties

When bringing equipment into a country where it will subsequently remain, it typically has to be declared and will be subject to import tax. This sum must either be factored into your budget, or avoided by obtaining a customs waiver.

2. Equipment and skills for digitising in the field

Patrick Sutherland

This chapter describes the technical equipment and essential skills required for copying documentary material in the field. The main focus is upon digitisation using cameras, although scanners are touched upon at the end of the chapter. The chapter begins by introducing the digital camera from first principles, outlining key technical aspects such as exposure, aperture, shutter speed and choice of lens. It then considers other essential equipment, including copy stands and tripods, relating these to a discussion of lighting and flash — a key consideration for document copying. Throughout, the emphasis is on how to successfully copy material to archival standards, digitising it for long-term preservation, even in remote, challenging and unusual circumstances.

Cameras and scanners

When specifying your project equipment, you will have a basic choice between a digital single lens reflex camera (DSLR) and a flatbed scanner for copying material to a professional standard. For very specific materials you may also need to consider a film scanner or overhead scanner, but these go beyond the scope of most EAP projects and neither is discussed further within this book. Both cameras and scanners have particular advantages and disadvantages. It is therefore essential to get a clear sense of the nature of the material you wish to copy, particularly its physical dimensions and character, together with the environment in which the copying will take place, before you make this choice and purchase equipment.

The importance of preparation

Whatever equipment you choose to purchase, it is **absolutely essential** that you get to know your copy set-up and are fully conversant with the technology prior to any field trip. This is true whether you are using a scanner or a digital camera with lenses, and whether you are using available light, supplementary lighting or flash. With camera technology and with flash, this learning process may take several days, especially if you have not used a sophisticated digital camera before. You also need to be fully conversant with your data management system.

Digital cameras and scanners are complex technologies and operating processes need to be learned well in advance of undertaking digitisation. This is especially true for projects in remote locations.

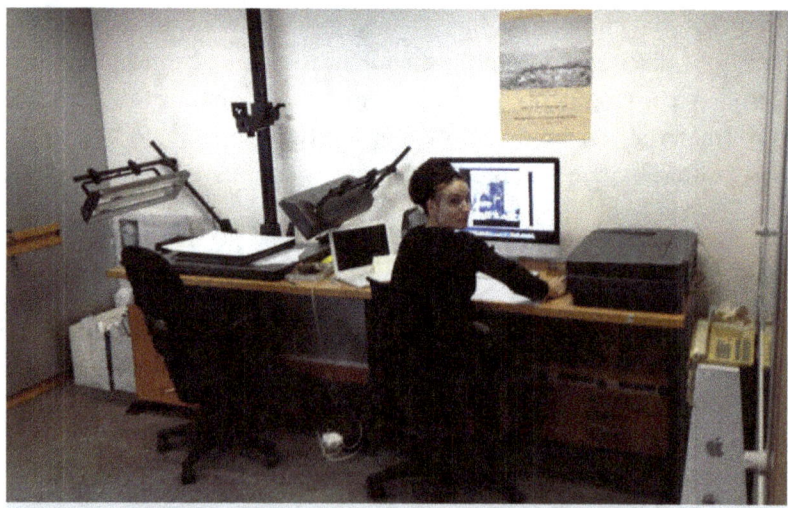

Figure 10. EAP644, Camera and scanner used in parallel, Beirut.
This project used both a camera with copy stand, and a scanner, to digitise nineteenth-century photographs.
Photo © Yasmine Chemali, CC BY 4.0.

Camera or scanner?

Advantages of scanners
- Flatbed scanners keep simple documents completely flat and illuminate them internally. They therefore avoid the problems of aligning documents and the potential distortion from using wide-angle lenses with cameras. Used correctly, the scanner produces images that are accurate facsimiles of the originals.
- Scanners can save files direct to TIFF format and can easily be set up to save files using the final EAP file names, thereby reducing the post-production workload.

Disadvantages of scanners
- Scanners have limitations on the maximum size of document they can copy.
- Scanners that will work with documents larger than A3 (29.7 x 42.0cm) are extremely expensive, very large and are not portable.
- Scanners are only appropriate in situations with a reliable electricity supply.
- Using scanners involves handling documents, as well as contact between the page and scanning platen. This is not always appropriate from a conservation standpoint, above all with bound materials.

Advantages of digital cameras
- Cameras are much faster to use than scanners when copying large numbers of documents of a similar size (pages of an unbound book or photographs of a standard size, for example).
- Cameras run off rechargeable batteries and are not directly dependent on electricity or connection to a computer, so are better suited to working in situations where electricity supplies are unpredictable. (Batteries need to be recharged, however, so some access to an electricity supply is essential.)

Disadvantages of digital cameras
- Digital cameras are significantly more complex to use than most scanners, so the learning curve is much steeper.
- Many cameras do not record in TIFF format, so files need to be exported from RAW to TIFF. Files will also need to be renamed during this process (see Chapter 6).
- Cameras have to be set up carefully to ensure that the camera back is parallel to the copying surface, so that the documents being copied are squared up and not distorted in the process. This is particularly true when using wide-angle lenses.

What camera brand should I buy?

Canon and Nikon are very well established camera brands, being the default choice of most professional photographers. They have a wide range of camera bodies, lenses, accessories and flashgun systems, and the cameras they produce in the semi-professional range are rugged and reliable and therefore very suitable for conditions in the field. Cheaper cameras in their ranges, though capable of producing excellent images, are perhaps less likely to survive the rigours of fieldwork. Their moisture and dust seals are less effective and their shutters will not last so long.

The Digital SLR camera: a general introduction

Digital cameras are devices which capture and store images in a digital format. They record the light passing through a lens onto a light-sensitive electronic sensor that captures a permanent image. There is a huge variety of different kinds of digital camera. They are now commonly built into phones, computers, tablets and many other devices. However, the Digital Single Lens Reflex is the ideal camera for copying because of the level of control it offers over framing, focus and exposure.

The Endangered Archive Programme only recommends the use of DSLR cameras and does not recommend the use of other kinds of camera.[1] As well as offering high image quality, the design of a DSLR camera allows the operator to see directly through the lens of the camera, rather than through a separate viewfinder. (This is true whether you are actually looking through the camera viewfinder or using the rear LCD screen.) This means that the framing and focussing of the camera is extremely accurate, which is especially important when copying close up. Equally importantly, DSLRs allow for very precise control of exposure when using available light or flash. They allow the photographer to view images almost immediately in order to check the quality of reproduction, the focus and exposure, and to assess the arrangement of objects within the frame and check for any problems like surface reflection. DSLRs can also be set up for tethered shooting, which entails connecting a digital camera to a computer. As described below, special tethering software displays the image onto the computer screen and can save the image files directly onto the computer hard drive and/or the camera's memory card. Finally, DSLRs have interchangeable lenses.

---

1   Digital camera technology is continually evolving, and manufacturers may well develop mirrorless camera technologies appropriate for digitisation projects in remote locations.

Full-frame or APS camera?

The term full frame is used by photographers as shorthand for an image sensor format which is the same size as 35mm format film (36 x 24mm). Historically, 35mm was considered a small film format compared with medium format or large format cameras.

Advanced Photo System (APS) sensor cameras have much smaller sensors (approximately 22.5 x 15mm, but varying between manufacturers). This means a full-frame sensor has over 2.25 times the surface area of an APS-C sensor.

Advantages of APS cameras
- Cheaper, slightly smaller and slightly lighter than full-frame cameras of similar build quality and specification.
- Good APS cameras produce high quality image files perfectly acceptable for EAP projects.

Disadvantages of APS
- The focal lengths of all lenses are effectively magnified by 1.5–1.6 times, meaning that a standard 50mm lens becomes a short telephoto lens. This can cause problems for projects copying larger items. (However, a good close-focussing 35–40mm fixed focal length lens could replace a 50mm macro for most copying of items larger than 12 x 18cm.)

Advantages of full-frame cameras
- Higher quality resulting from the larger sensor size.
- No magnification of lens focal length.

Disadvantages of full-frame cameras
- More expensive than APS cameras of similar quality. They also tend to be larger and heavier. Cheaper full-framed cameras offer excellent image quality but are less robust than more expensive cameras.

For more on recommended cameras, see Digital Appendix 4 at https://doi.org/10.11647/OBP.0138.11

DSLRs: principles and settings

Exposure

The exposure is a measure of the amount of light that is transmitted through the camera lens to the sensor. This is the light reflected from the surfaces of the objects framed by the camera.

In any given lighting situation, correct exposure is achieved through setting a combination of the aperture and shutter speed at a particular ISO setting. These settings are recorded in the metadata attached to each digital file. In simple terms, the ISO setting represents the sensitivity of the camera to light. Therefore, and as discussed below, the larger the ISO number the more sensitive it is. Changing any of these three variables of aperture, shutter speed and ISO changes the exposure. (The exception is when working with flash, where in many situations changing the shutter speed has little or no effect on exposure.)

The aperture

Camera lenses contain an aperture, which is essentially a hole through which light can travel. The diameter of this aperture is adjustable in much the same way that the iris of an eye adjusts the size of the pupil. On most DSLRs the aperture is adjusted on the camera, rather than on the lens.

The aperture controls the amount of light that passes through the lens, thereby affecting the sensor's exposure to light. Aperture settings are expressed as f-numbers. Smaller apertures have larger f-numbers (f16 for example), whilst larger apertures have smaller f-numbers (e.g. f2.8). On older lenses the aperture was controlled by a ring engraved with numbers in the following order: f1.4, f2, f2.8, f4, f5.6, f8, f11, f16, f22. (In this example, the maximum aperture of this particular lens is f1.4 and the minimum is f22: maximum and minimum apertures vary between different kinds of lenses.) The difference between each adjacent aperture number on this list is known by photographers as a 'stop'.

'Opening up' the aperture by one stop, from say f5.6 to f4, doubles the amount of light that passes through the lens. In contrast, 'closing down' the aperture by one stop, for example from f8 to f11, halves the amount of light that passes through the lens. On DSLRs you can adjust the aperture in increments of a third of a stop. Because of the way that f-numbers are calculated, an aperture setting of f8 will yield the same exposure with different lenses, providing that other parameters are identical.

The aperture also affects the depth of field of the image: as discussed below, smaller aperture settings (i.e. higher f-numbers) have a greater depth of field. As a general rule of thumb, you should be copying with a minimum aperture setting of f8, so settings of f11 or f16 are also fine. Settings beyond these, such as f22, are not as sharp for most lenses. These settings will give you better depth of field than using the lens wide open and therefore tends to keep the image sharper from corner to corner of the frame. It also results in sharper images of items that are not completely flat — for example, a thick, tightly bound book, where the gutter may be a little closer to the camera than the outer edge of the page.

Regardless of the aperture you have chosen, you should always examine the results to check sharpness by zooming into the image displayed on the rear LCD screen or by checking on a computer screen. Check the sharpness of the image in the corners as well as in the centre.

The shutter

The shutter is a curtain-like device in front of the camera sensor, which remains closed until a photograph is taken. When the camera shutter is fired, the shutter opens for a determined period of time (the shutter speed), exposing the sensor to light passing through the lens.

The shutter speed controls the time that the sensor is exposed to the light that passes through the lens. Traditionally, shutter speeds were set at speeds of 1 second (sec), 1/2 sec, 1/4sec, 1/8 sec, 1/15 sec, 1/30 sec, 1/60 sec, 1/125 sec, 1/250 sec, and 1/500 sec, but modern shutters now also have much faster and slower speeds. As in the example of apertures, the difference between each of these speeds is one 'stop'. Changing the shutter speed from, say, 1/30 to 1/60, reduces the time that the shutter is open and the sensor is exposed to light by a factor of two, halving the exposure. Changing from 1/4 sec to 1/2 sec increases the time that the shutter is open and the sensor is exposed to light, doubling the exposure. (On DSLRs you can adjust the shutter speed in increments of one third of a stop.)

Shutter speed also affects the sharpness of the image. Fast shutter speeds are primarily important to freeze movement and to reduce the impact of camera shake. However, it is essential to use either a copy stand or a tripod for professional copying of still documents. Consequently, provided there are no other sources of vibration (passing traffic, vibrating equipment in the room or on the table such as fans), slow shutter speeds are not a problem and should not affect sharpness. As described below, to reduce the possibility of vibrations even further we recommend using a remote release or tethered shooting to trigger the shutter.

ISO settings

ISO stands for International Standards Organisation. In photography, it refers to a standardised measurement of how sensitive the camera sensor is to light. Along with the aperture and shutter speed settings, the ISO setting plays a very specific role in exposure. On lower ISO settings, the sensor is less sensitive to light; on higher ISO settings, the sensor is more sensitive to light. Importantly, the lower the ISO setting, the higher the quality of the images created on the sensor. Higher ISO settings are subject to increasing levels of digital noise, which affects the image quality. This 'noise' equates to the graininess of films using high ASA (film speed) settings — though digital noise seems less aesthetically acceptable than graininess.

As a good general rule, you should use an ISO setting of 100 or 200. Do not use an ISO setting above 400.

Setting the exposure

In any given lighting condition at a particular ISO setting, correct exposure is achieved by the *combination* of aperture and shutter speed. This varies the amount of light transmitted onto the sensor: the correct combination of aperture and shutter speed allows sufficient light onto the sensor to achieve correct exposure.

For example, if you are copying documents using available light (i.e. not flash) at ISO 100 and correct exposure is achieved at a setting of 1/60 sec at f5.6, then the same overall exposure will be achieved by combinations of 1/125 at f4, 1/250 at f2.8 or 1/500 at f2, or alternatively 1/30 at f8, 1/15 at f11 or 1/8 at f16. In such situations, shutter speed and aperture setting have a reciprocal relationship: if you change one you have to change the other to maintain identical exposure. If you are photographing a completely flat object using a copy stand so there is no subject movement, then the images produced at each of these settings should look identical.

Exposure modes

Semi-professional digital SLRs offer a range of exposure modes, commonly selected via a dial on the top of the camera:

- **Aperture Priority** (the letter A on a Nikon, Av on a Canon): in this automated exposure mode, the photographer chooses the ISO setting and the aperture, and the camera computes the shutter speed needed to give correct exposure.

- **Manual** (the letter M on both Nikon and Canon): in manual exposure mode, the photographer chooses the ISO setting as well as the shutter speed and the aperture needed to achieve correct exposure.

- **Shutter Speed Priority** (the letter S on a Nikon, Tv on a Canon): in this automated exposure mode, the photographer chooses the ISO setting and the shutter speed, and the camera computes the aperture needed to give correct exposure.

- **Programme Auto** (the letter P on both Nikon and Canon): in this automated exposure mode, the camera chooses the ISO setting, the shutter speed and the aperture needed to give correct exposure.

☐ Additionally, some cameras have other exposure settings and also allow for customisable settings. We do not recommend any for copying, and they should be ignored.

The development of digital camera technology has been concentrated on increasing automation, and auto modes on cameras are now extremely accurate. Most DSLRs can operate almost like point-and-shoot cameras and give remarkably good results in terms of focus and exposure. However, digital cameras cannot make the very specific kind of decisions that are needed when copying to professional standards. For that reason, and for all but the most competent photographers, we recommend using **Aperture Priority exposure**, i.e. setting the aperture and ISO first, then letting the camera work out the exposure according to the lighting conditions, whether available light or flash. Alternatively, but only if you are experienced and technically proficient, you can work using the manual exposure setting, in which case you should set the aperture and ISO first then work out the exposure and shutter speed setting yourself, according to the lighting conditions.

Setting up the camera

Settings
- Set the camera to shoot in RAW format (NOT sRAW, mRAW or JPEG).
- Set the colour space to sRGB.
- Set picture style to Neutral.
- Switch on the highlight alert feature to indicate any over-exposed areas.
- Switch on the electronic grid to aid composition and squaring up the image (or replace the focussing screen with a grid screen).

Using the rear LCD screen

The LCD screen on the back of the camera can display all the key information (the selected shutter speed, aperture, ISO setting, choice of RAW settings, choice of manual or auto exposure settings, picture style, white balance, exposure compensation, battery levels, number of frames remaining etc.). Most of this information is also visible through the viewfinder or on the top LCD screen but is much more easily read on the main LCD screen. Many of these key settings can also be easily and quickly adjusted here rather than accessing key settings through other menus or dials.

Get used to checking the displayed settings prior to each shooting session and double-checking regularly to make certain no settings have been accidentally changed. Some cameras allow you to lock the settings and thus prevent unintentional changes.

Using the Aperture Priority mode

Fix the camera on a tripod or copy stand. Put the camera into Aperture Priority mode (the A setting on Nikon, the Av setting on Canon). **Set the ISO to 100 and the aperture to f8 or smaller (f11 or f16).** Carefully arrange the material within the frame, including the colour checker/measure. Focus the lens, adjusting the height of the camera up the copy stand column if necessary. Shoot the image using a remote release. The camera will automatically compute the correct shutter speed and apply it. (N.B. The settings will be displayed in the camera viewfinder and/or the LCD rear screen.) Next, examine the results:

- ☐ Check the quality of reproduction: confirm that the material being copied is in focus and correctly exposed.
- ☐ Check for sharpness from corner to corner. If the image is generally in focus but one side falls out of focus, check that the camera back is parallel to the surface of the material being copied and that the material is flat. If the corners are falling out of focus, then try shooting at a smaller aperture.
- ☐ Check for problems like surface reflection and adjust the lighting if necessary.

- ☐ Check the evenness of the lighting across the frame and any fall-off in the corners and adjust the lighting if necessary.
- ☐ Check for any colour cast,[2] a tint caused by mixed lighting, most visible in white areas, and adjust the lighting if necessary.
- ☐ Double check the arrangement of objects within the frame.
- ☐ Reshoot if required.

In order to check the quality of the image, you should ideally view the image on a computer screen, but if necessary use the camera's rear LCD screen to view the histogram; also to zoom in on the images to check focus, overall sharpness, exposure and colour balance.

Aperture Priority mode gives remarkably good results under most conditions. However, the camera will not always give perfect exposure in automatic settings. The built-in light meter in a camera assumes that the subject matter averages out as a mid-tone, and in most situations this works well, but when faced with subjects that are either much paler or darker in tone, images may be incorrectly exposed.

Incorrect exposure in the Aperture Priority mode can easily be modified using the exposure compensation control. Shift the exposure towards the + sign to make the image lighter and towards the − sign to make the image darker. Exposure compensation settings will be displayed in the viewfinder and on the rear LCD panel. When copying a large collection of objects of a similar tone — paper documents or book pages, for example — you may well find that you use a particular level of exposure compensation repeatedly, setting it as a default compensation for files that would otherwise be incorrectly exposed. But remember to check the exposure regularly during such long copying sessions and reset the exposure compensation to zero when you have finished digitising that group of materials.

Correct exposure gives full detail in both the shadow (darker) areas and the highlight (lighter) areas of the image. Underexposure leads to a loss of detail in the shadow areas of the image; overexposure leads to a loss of detail in the highlight areas of the image.

---

2 A colour cast is a tint of a particular colour, which is usually unwanted, and which affects the photographic image.

> It is vital that you check your images thoroughly, and as soon as possible after you have taken them. Having to reshoot is an irritation, but it is far better done straight away — rather than having to retrieve a book from an archive, or worse, having to revisit a remote site.

Using the Manual exposure mode

Fix the camera on a tripod or copy stand. Put the camera into Manual exposure mode (the M setting on both Nikon and Canon cameras). **Set the aperture to f8 or smaller and the ISO to 100.** Carefully arrange the material within the frame including the colour chart/measure. Focus the lens, adjusting the height of the camera up the copy stand column if necessary. Adjust the shutter speed until the exposure indicator in the camera viewfinder is centred, indicating correct exposure. Shoot the photograph using a remote release. Then examine the results as per the Aperture Priority instructions above.

N.B. On manual settings, you cannot use the exposure compensation control. Instead, the exposure can easily be modified by changing the shutter speed, choosing a slower speed to make the image lighter and a faster speed to make the image darker.

What is depth of field?

When you focus the lens on something in front of a camera, you are establishing a plane of focus that is parallel to the back of the camera. Anything in that plane will also be in focus. The distance between the nearest and furthest objects in front of, or behind, this plane of focus that are also acceptably sharp is known as the depth of field. Depth of field increases as you make the aperture smaller and reduces as you make the aperture larger. So, all other things being equal, a lens has greater depth of field set at f11 than set at f4. Depth of field also reduces as you focus closer to the camera and increases as you focus further away, i.e. changing the separation between the camera and the object(s) being photographed.

The most important consideration when copying is to keep the subject matter as flat as possible, so that it is in focus from corner to corner. Shutting the aperture down will increase the depth of field slightly and therefore help to keep the edges of the material in focus.

Depth of field and close-up photography

As a good general rule, you should use an aperture of f8 or smaller.

If your material is very flat then a setting of f8 is probably fine, but if the material is three-dimensional and especially if it is also small, so that you are working very close, then a smaller aperture setting is recommended for maximum depth of field and image sharpness. In these situations, depth of field will be extremely shallow. To try to get the sharpest image, use the smallest aperture possible and focus very carefully. Try taking more than one exposure if necessary, focussing on different planes of the object; focus partway between the nearest and furthest surface of the object and select the sharpest frame when you can carefully compare them on the computer.

Use the LCD screen to double-check image sharpness on a regular basis.

Reading histograms

Digital cameras allow you to view the exposure given to any photograph in the form of a histogram. The histogram is a visual display in graph-like format of the image's tonal range. It represents a scale from black to white and shows whether the frame is correctly exposed, underexposed (too dark) or overexposed (too light). It is a good idea to regularly check the histograms. You can view them on the camera's rear LCD screen immediately after shooting an image.

The far left of the histogram represents pure black, and the far right represents pure white. The middle of the histogram represents mid-tones. If the subject matter consists primarily of mid-tones — a mid-brown document on a mid-grey background for example — then the histogram should display as a peak in the middle of the scale. If it is primarily composed of darker tones then the histogram will display as

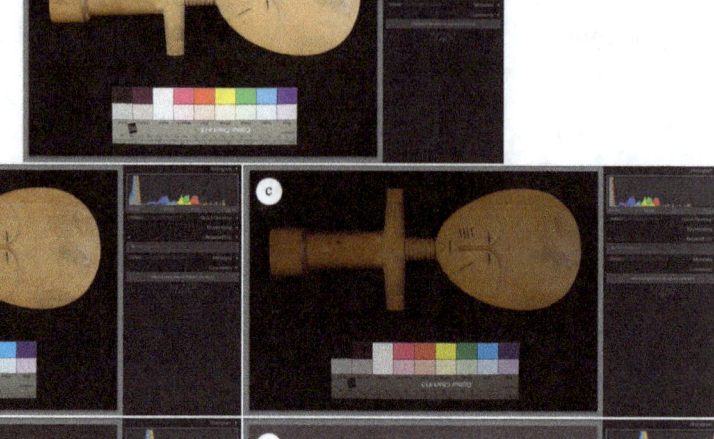

Figure 11. Example histograms.
(a) Correct exposure with centred histogram. (b) Slight underexposure with non-centred histogram ranged left. (c) Underexposure with histogram clipping on the left and loss of shadow detail. (d) Slight overexposure with non-centred histogram ranged right. (e) Overexposure with histogram clipping on the right and loss of highlight detail. Photos © Patrick Sutherland, CC BY 4.0.

a peak on the left of the scale. If it is primarily composed of paler tones then the histogram will display as a peak on the right of the scale. If the histogram runs off the left or right of the scale then the histogram is 'clipped', meaning that part of the digital information is lost. If the image is underexposed then the histogram will run off the left-hand edge of the scale, indicating loss of detail in the shadow areas, the darker tones. If the image is overexposed then the histogram will run off the right-hand edge of the scale, indicating loss of detail in the highlight areas, the paler tones. This information from the histogram will reflect the qualities of the image displayed on the LCD screen (or on the computer screen). Ideally the exposure should be set so that the histogram does not run off either side of the scale.

Every histogram will look different, as some subjects are much lighter in tone and others much darker, and therefore correct exposure will reflect this variation. The height of the histogram at any point along the scale indicates the amount of data of that specific tone within the image. **There is no such thing as an average looking histogram.**

White balance and shooting in mixed lighting conditions

Sources of light, like the sun in the early morning or late evening, the sky on an overcast day, fluorescent tubes or household tungsten lights, emit light of a certain colour temperature, which is not the same as 'white' light. Our brains process the information that comes through our eyes, and compensate for variations in the colour temperature of the light around us. Consequently, we normally see the colours of objects 'correctly' in whatever light we view them. In other words, we see them without colour casts. But cameras have to be set up to remove the casts that would otherwise occur when shooting in different lighting conditions.

Digital cameras have an automatic white balance setting, which will adjust the colour temperature of the image to take into account the colour of the light falling on the material being copied. For most situations, setting auto white balance on the camera will result in a very close approximation to correct and natural looking colour: i.e. as if the light source illuminating the material is pure white light. More precise colour balancing can be done later if necessary, using the colour chart as a reference point. When shooting in RAW, the files can be easily adjusted after shooting as the RAW file is essentially unprocessed. Use the image processing software that comes with the camera or import the files into a programme like Adobe Lightroom.

However, this auto white balance (AWB) cannot work when light sources are mixed: for example, where the subject is being illuminated by both natural daylight and artificial light. In such mixed lighting, images will pick up colour casts that cannot be removed. To avoid this problem, don't photograph in mixed lighting. Shoot either by available electric lights of one kind, or in daylight, but don't mix the two. (Keep away from windows if you are shooting by domestic lighting; turn off

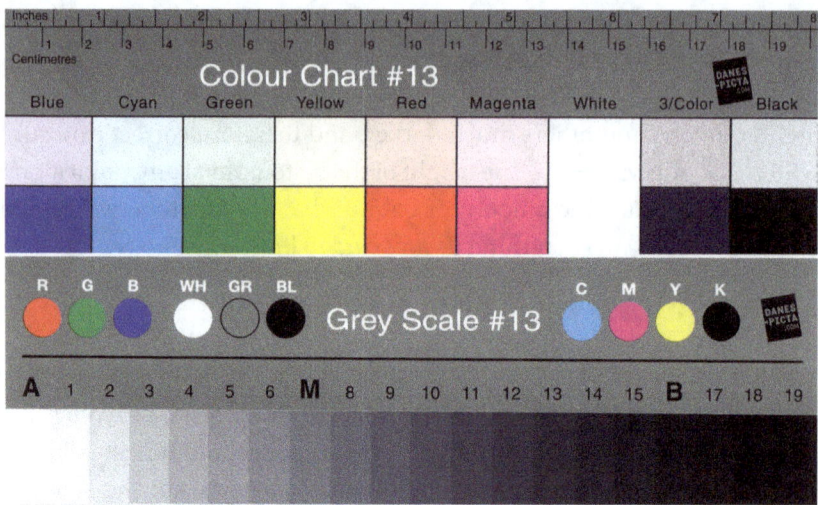

Figure 12. Greyscale and colour checker.
Photo © Patrick Sutherland, CC BY 4.0.

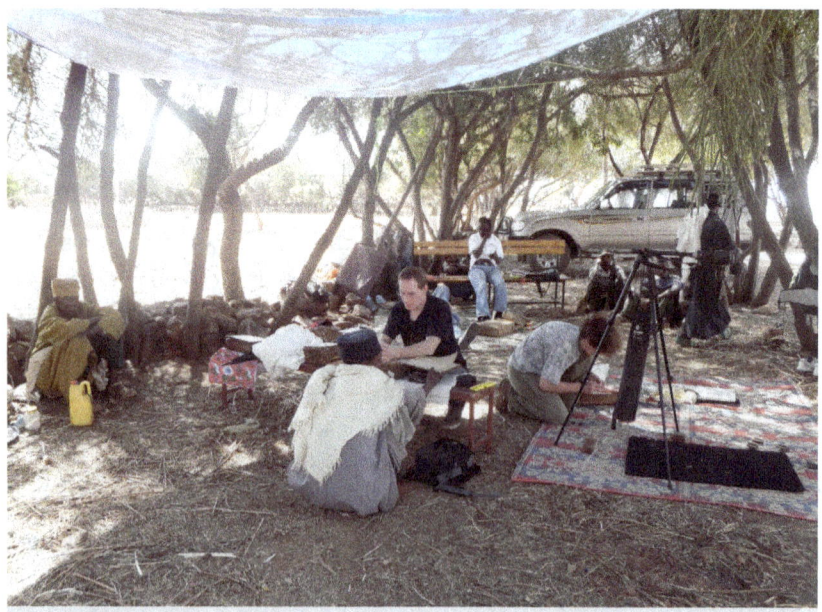

Figure 13. EAP704 Däbrä Abbay and EAP526 May Wäyni, Ethiopia.
Digitising in the open air, inside a tent, to prevent harsh sunlight.
Photo © Michael Gervers, CC BY 4.0.

the household lights if you are shooting by diffuse daylight or flash.) Different kinds of indoor lighting give different coloured light sources: do not mix fluorescent and other kinds of electric lighting. A coloured wall will reflect light of that colour and may cause a colour cast if it is too near to the copy set-up: move the camera away or cover the wall with a white sheet.

If you are shooting all your work under particular lighting conditions (e.g. fluorescent tubes) and find that the files have a colour cast even when using the AWB setting, then you can change the camera's white balance control manually to a different setting. Cameras have a list of pre-set settings under the white balance menu, or you can adjust the colour temperature manually.

When shooting in daylight you should also avoid shooting in direct sunlight as this harsh lighting will produce very strong shadows. Shoot instead in the shade or perhaps inside a white tent. A white sheet will turn harsh sunlight into a soft and diffuse light source. Reflectors consisting of white sheets or sheets of white card can even out and soften harsh direct lighting.

Colour calibration using colour checkers

As well as preserving documentary information, the aim of EAP digitisation is also to record the physical artefact itself; this is the case whether it was designed with aesthetic qualities in mind (for example, a decorated scroll or illuminated manuscript) or was a working document whose original purpose was solely utilitarian.

Accurate reproduction of colour is therefore an important factor, and this is achieved by the inclusion of a greyscale and colour separation guide within each photograph (abbreviated to 'colour checker' in this book). This checker contains a number of colour squares, graduated across the colour spectrum, alongside graduated greyscale that spans light to dark tones. A size measurement scale is also present.

The presence of the checker in the photograph means that the original tonal values of the document can be correctly reproduced.[3] Regardless of what lighting conditions you had to work with, and how your

---

3   In this book we have called this a colour checker; it can also be referred to as a colour separation or colour calibration card.

photograph appears on the camera LED screen or on different computer screens, it will always be possible to work out what the correct colour of your original document was. Developing software uses the information from the checker to enable these colours to be exactly replicated on properly calibrated screens, in exported files and in print-outs.

> ## Digital file formats
>
> RAW files generated by digital cameras store uncompressed image data exactly as it was captured by the camera, containing data from the sensor that has been minimally processed and with minimal loss of information. They need to be processed by a software programme, an image-editing RAW converter, before saving in a file format such as TIFF for storage or for printing. In the process of converting RAW files they can be adjusted significantly: for example, for white balance and exposure.
>
> All camera brands use their own proprietary RAW format (.NEF files for Nikon and .CR2 files for Canon). RAW files are larger than JPEGs but significantly smaller than the TIFF files they generate.
>
> TIFF files are commonly used in the printing industry and are much larger than their JPEG equivalents, because they are uncompressed or compressed using lossless compression.
>
> JPEG files are a common photographic file format much smaller than those files saved as TIFF, because they have been compressed. This compression loses information, hence their unsuitability for archival or documentary purposes.

Shooting in RAW

DSLR cameras allow you to record images in RAW and/or JPEG formats. **It is essential that you record in RAW at the largest file size.** (Canon, for example, offers the choice of RAW, MRAW and SRAW formats: the latter two are processed and compressed versions and should be avoided.)

Rules

- Always shoot in RAW at the maximum size. Do NOT shoot only in JPEG format.
- Set the camera to Av or Manual.
- ISO 100–200 is the ideal. Do not exceed ISO 400.

Choice of lens

Copying is a very particular kind of photography. It is important to choose appropriate lenses to correspond with the scale and nature of the material being copied. The ideal lens for most copying is a 'standard' lens and has a focal length of about 50mm (37mm on an APS camera). Nikon and Canon lenses such as these are quite small, very simple, often inexpensive, and very sharp. They also have a very natural and neutral perspective.

A 50mm standard lens (not a macro 50mm lens) on a full-frame DSLR camera will usually focus down to about 50cm and cover an area of about 18 x 27cm. Some standard lenses will focus even closer. All standard lenses can be used for general copying but some, unlike proper macro lenses, will cause noticeable distortion of the image at very close working distances.

If you are regularly dealing with material smaller than this then a macro lens is essential. These lenses are optically designed for close-up photography and mechanically designed to focus from infinity down to half life-size or even closer. They are also very sharp. It is important to note that the exposure changes as you focus very close up, so check the results regularly. If you are copying a lot of very small material then a longer than normal macro lens (e.g. 100mm) will allow you to photograph very close up but maintain a greater distance between the end of the lens and the subject, causing fewer problems with shadows falling onto the subject.

A basic rule of copying is that if there is too much space around the object then move the camera closer (rather than zooming in); if you want more space around the object then move the camera further away (rather than zooming out). If you have a zoom lens attached to the camera, then the tendency is always to zoom in and out rather than moving the camera. This is obviously quicker than moving the camera but it is very easy to slip into photographing larger documents with a very wide-angle setting. To avoid this tendency and to establish an efficient workflow, you could arrange the material being copied by size, photographing objects of a similar size together in batches so that the camera is moved less frequently. Wide-angle lenses or the wide-angle settings on a zoom lens should only be used for copying when there is no alternative as they are more likely to introduce distortion into the image. This is particularly true with cheaper zoom lenses.

However, there are situations when using a wide-angle lens or using a zoom on a wide-angle setting becomes unavoidable. In such circumstances you must take special care to make sure that the back of the camera is parallel to the surface being copied otherwise the image will show obvious distortion.

Try to use the zoom on a standard lens setting (approximately 50mm on a full-frame DSLR, approximately 37mm on an APS camera) and move the camera up and down to frame and reframe: try to avoid using the zoom facility and especially try to avoid using settings wider than 35mm (24mm on an APS camera).

If you do purchase a zoom lens, check that the lens does not shift focus or change focal length and zoom in when held pointing downwards. Some lenses do this even when brand new and this is infuriating when copying. Lenses with internal focussing mechanisms are less liable to exhibit this phenomenon of 'lens creep', though the focussing mechanism of well-used lenses becomes looser and more liable to this movement. (If the focus or focal length does shift you will need to tape up the lens barrel to prevent this.)

Wherever possible, use lenses made by the manufacturer of your camera. They are designed to function together seamlessly. However, some independent manufacturers like Sigma make very high quality lenses that are fully compatible with all functions of Nikon or Canon digital cameras.

Focussing in low light/manual focus

If you are working in low light levels and the camera finds accurate focussing difficult then switch the lens to manual focussing. Place a piece of paper that contains sharp graphic information (a newspaper headline, for example) on the baseboard and use that to fix the focus.

Framing and squaring up images

Many DSLR cameras have electronic framing grids that can be activated from one of the digital menus. Some cameras have changeable focussing screens that achieve the same purpose. These simple rectilinear grids appear in the camera viewfinder and/or LCD screen and help simplify the process of squaring up images. In order for the image to be perfectly squared up, the camera has to be pointing at 90 degrees to the copy area and the back of the camera has to be parallel to the baseboard/copy surface. The copy surface and camera back don't necessarily need to be perfectly horizontal, but should be perfectly parallel to each other. An inexpensive digital level can be used to simply align the camera back to match the copy surface or baseboard.

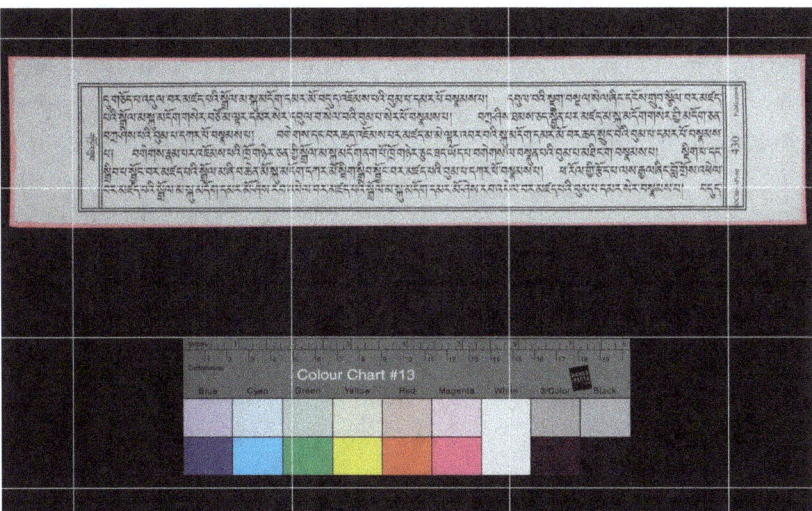

Figure 14. Electronic grids assist with the alignment of objects when copying. Photo © Patrick Sutherland, CC BY 4.0.

Tripods, copy stands and remote controls

Use of a tripod or copy stand is essential when photographing archival material. Tripods and copy stands hold the camera still and, provided they are not subject to movement or vibration, will minimise camera shake. Such supports help to achieve very sharp images even with low level ambient light exposures when slower shutter speeds are common and camera shake most likely. But equally importantly these supports allow the photographer to precisely control the framing of the material being copied, and to fix the focussing in low light conditions.

Remote controls

When mounted on a tripod or copy stand, the camera can be operated conventionally, with the user manually selecting all the settings on the camera itself, via the physical dials and the on-screen menus. The actual photograph can be taken by directly pressing the shutter button. However, while this is a perfectly acceptable approach in normal photography, it has disadvantages when digitising. Firstly, it is difficult to press the shutter button on the camera without introducing some element of 'camera shake', particularly when using slow shutter speeds. Secondly, to manually operate the camera you clearly have to be standing next to it. This is not always practical if the camera is mounted high up on a copy stand or tripod. Moreover, if working on your own, you may also need your hands to hold down or steady your manuscript!

Using a remote control/remote shutter release will help to avoid camera shake. It can also speed up the copying process. Using a copy set-up with a rigidly mounted camera and a remote control allows for rapid copying of a series of identically sized objects (unbound book pages, for example). These accessories allow you to trigger the camera shutter without having to touch the camera. They come in two kinds. Wireless remote controls like the Nikon ML-L3 or Canon RC-6 operate on a wireless or infra-red signal and, provided the camera has been set up to accept this signal, will trigger the shutter from up to 5m away. The remote has to be pointing at the camera. All such units require a battery.

Other remote controls like the Canon RS-80N3 are cables connected to a special camera port. They still require you to be close to the camera and you have to be careful to keep the cable loose so that the camera is not pulled when the exposure is made. (N.B. Check which specific remote works with the camera model you have chosen to purchase.) Some of these non-wireless remotes operate without a battery.

Tethered shooting

A further alternative is to use camera tethered shooting, where the camera is triggered from a computer. Tethered shooting is a more advanced form of remote control. Here, the camera is linked to, and operated almost entirely from, a computer. The camera is connected via a cable to the computer's USB port, hence 'tethering'. Operation of the camera is via a software program: Nikon's Camera Control Pro has to be purchased separately, but Canon's excellent EOS Utility comes free with its cameras. Other commercial software will perform the same function, including Adobe Lightroom.

In tethered shooting, the only time the camera needs to be touched is to set the physical dial for exposure mode (Aperture Priority or Manual) and, if using a zoom lens, the focal length also has to be set manually. All other functions are performed remotely, while tools such as histograms are also accessible on-screen.

Tethering has the advantages of remote shutter releases, and more:

- You can record images to the camera's memory card, directly to the computer hard drive, or to both simultaneously. If you record to both card and computer, you will have already made a second copy of your images (i.e. an instant backup).

- Assuming your camera has a Live View function, the image you are about to take will be visible on your computer screen. What you see is what you will get, and if adjustments are needed (for example to framing), these can be made before taking the photograph.[4]

---

4 If photographing using Live View *and* flash, on Canon cameras you will need to disable 'exposure simulation' (which is enabled by default). Otherwise, because the camera does not know you are using flash, it will show exactly what you would get with your aperture and exposure settings if relying on ambient light — which is likely to be nothing but a black image. By disabling exposure simulation, the Live View function will amplify the ambient light to provide an image that can be used for composition and focusing. If using Nikon Capture One tethering software, there is a button on the Live View display that allows the user to toggle between these two ways of using Live View.

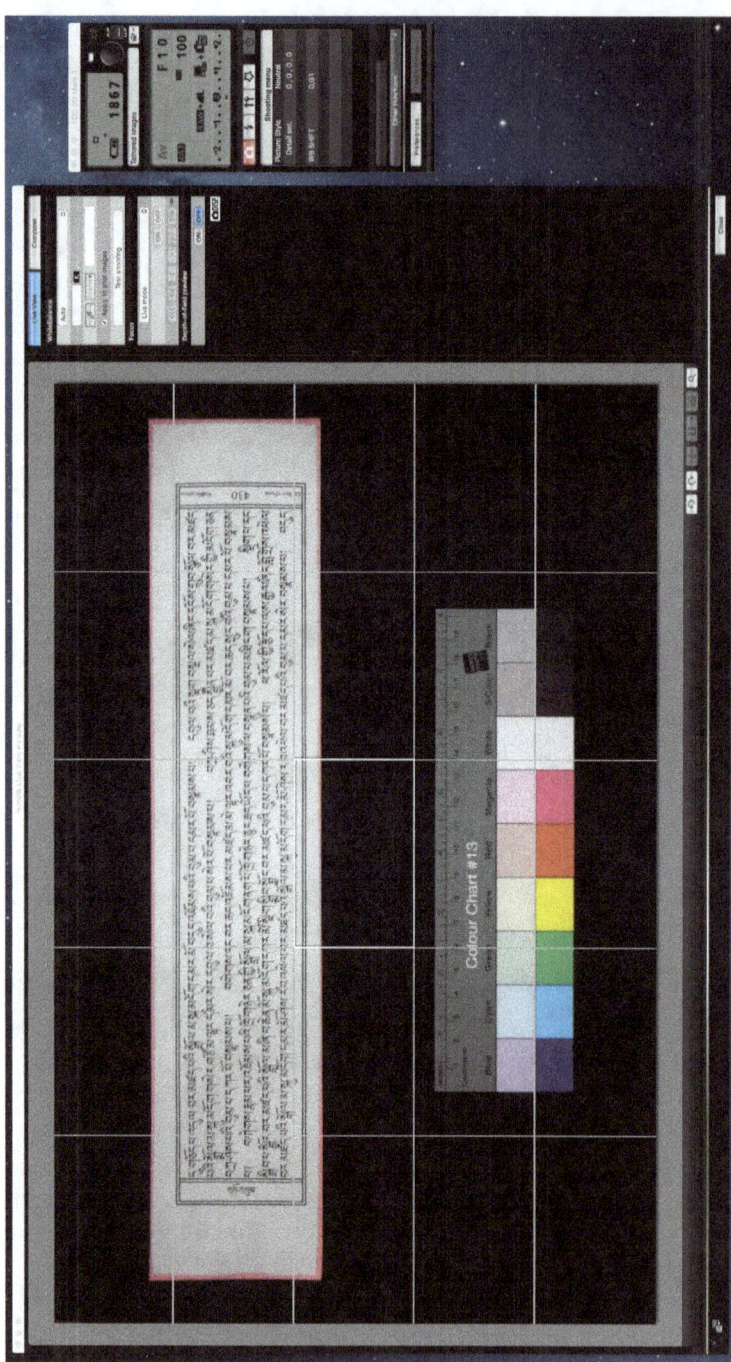

Figure 15. EOS Utility. Photo © Patrick Sutherland, CC BY 4.0.

☐ Photographs can be reviewed on your computer immediately after they have been taken. You do not need to rely on the camera's own small screen, which in any case may be awkwardly high up on a camera stand.

Copy stands

Copy stands have significant advantages over tripods in that they are designed specifically for copying. They are easier to set up and more stable, and it is much easier to get the camera exactly parallel to the baseboard on a good copy stand than on a tripod. They consist of a vertical column attached to a rigid base. A moveable arm attached to the column allows the user to position the camera directly above the baseboard and vary the height of the camera to take account of the dimensions of the material being copied. A portable spirit level will help check that the camera back is positioned parallel to the baseboard. **The height of the column determines the maximum size of item to be copied.**

With a 50mm macro lens on a full-frame DSLR, a copy stand with a 70cm column will allow copying of material from approximately 5 x 7.5cm to approximately 28 x 42cm. The rigid base makes copy stands less portable than tripods, though the column can be detached from the baseboard for transportation. Lack of portability is less of an issue if all the copying will take place within one institution.

Some DSLRs have tilting LCD screens. Tilting screens are very useful when copying with the camera on a copy stand, when the height of the camera can often make viewing a fixed LCD screen or through a normal viewfinder awkward.

There are clearly limitations to the copy stand: the maximum height of the column is one, but there is also the problem that when using the camera high up a long column (over 75cm) you may start to include the base of the column in the frame. Up to a point, you can compensate for this problem by extending the distance between the camera and column. Some models have extension arms to help overcome this issue.

Kaiser is a well-established brand and supplies a modular range of copy stands: you can choose the height of the column, the size of the

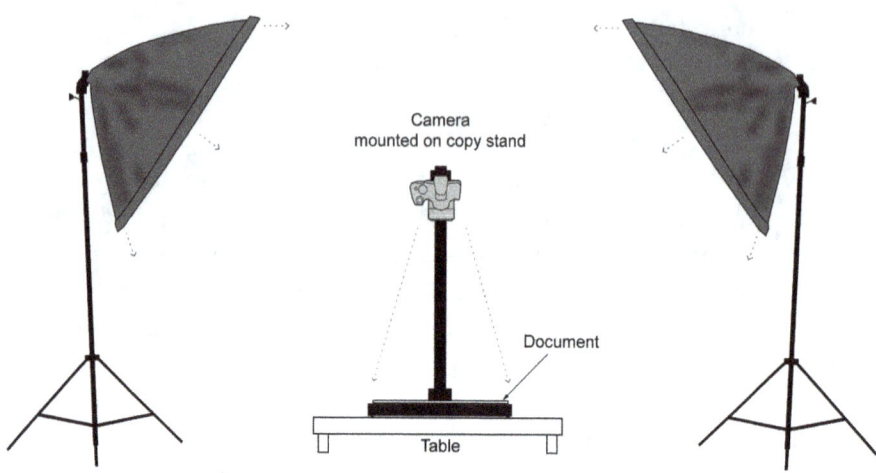

Figure 16. Copy stand with angled lights. Illustration © Anne Leaver, CC BY 4.0.

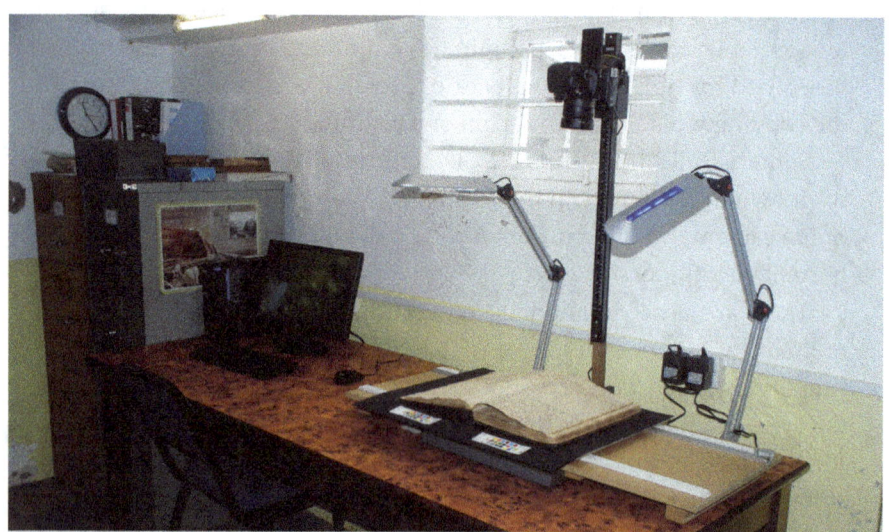

Figure 17. EAP524, Camera and copy stand in situ in the St Helena Government Archives. Photo © Andrew Pearson, CC BY 4.0.

baseboard and the kind of lights attached. Some are quite portable, with others much heavier duty. Columns are detachable for transportation. Some smaller copy stands are available in portable kits, but always consider whether the column will be high enough for your needs.

It is usually possible to swivel the column of copy stands by 180 degrees or to mount the moveable arm in reversed position. It is then possible to use a copy stand to photograph much larger objects: position the copy stand on the edge of a firm table with the camera pointing to a low table or the floor. It is **absolutely essential** in this situation to heavily weigh down the base of the copy stand as this arrangement is otherwise very unstable.

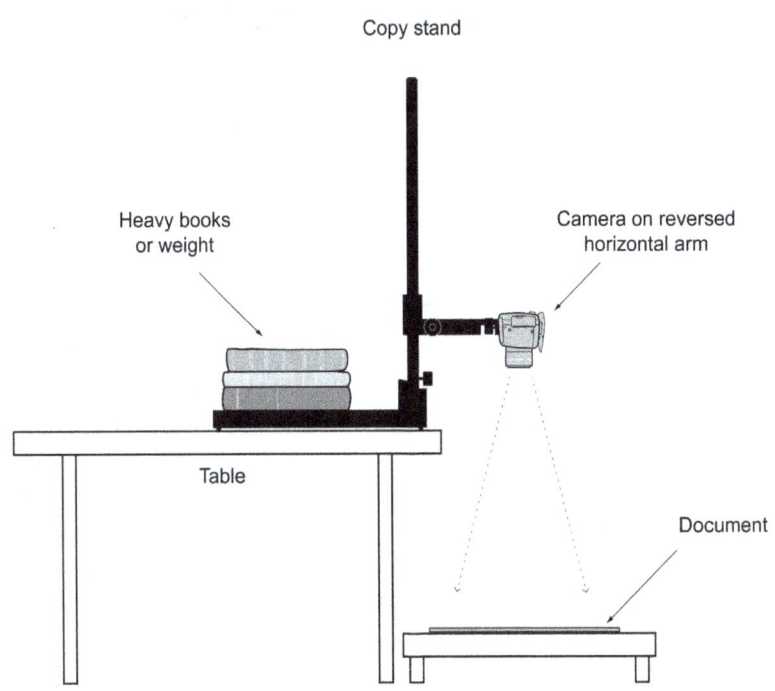

Figure 18. Diagram of copy stand in reversed position.
Illustration © Anne Leaver, CC BY 4.0.

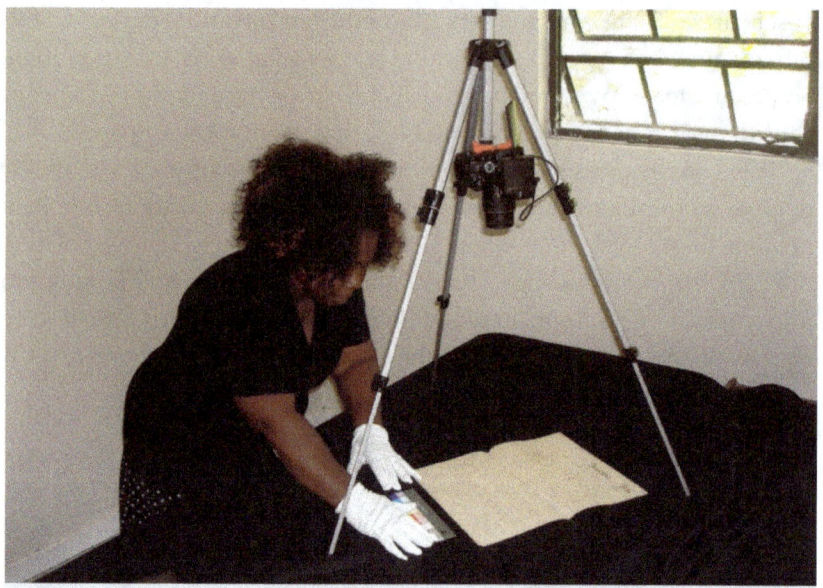

Figure 19. EAP769, Digitising using a tripod with camera attached to reversed centre column in Montserrat. Photo © Nigel Sadler, CC BY 4.0.

Tripods

An alternative to using a copy stand is a tripod. This may be a better choice if you are copying in many different situations and portability is a major issue. However, tripods are significantly harder to set up so that the camera and subject are perfectly squared up. There are hundreds of tripods on the market. A crude rule is that the heavier the tripod, the more stable it is likely to be, but of course the heavier it is, the less portable it is. You can add to the rigidity of a lighter tripod by weighing it down: some tripods have a hook at the bottom of the centre column to facilitate this. Make sure any weight attached is not left hanging free, as it could potentially swing like a pendulum and cause camera shake.

Tripods are excellent for copying items that are vertical or near-vertical. They are more awkward when used like a copy stand with the camera pointed downwards, because the camera and object have to fit between the tripod legs. You can reverse the centre column and place the camera close to the ground but that is also awkward. Some tripods allow for the angle of the legs to be varied, which makes copying easier.

All tripods with a removable tripod head can be fitted with a horizontal copy arm (e.g. those made by Manfrotto and Gitzo) which positions the camera away from the centre of the tripod. (You will need to remove the tripod head and fit the copy arm to the tripod's centre column and then refit the tripod head at the end of the copy arm.) Importantly, positioning the camera on a horizontal copy arm places the weight off-centre and makes the whole camera/tripod set-up very unstable. This must be counterbalanced to avoid it tipping over and damaging equipment: loop a cord over the other end of the copy arm and weigh it down.

Some tripods have an off-centre column as standard. These can be used vertically like a normal centre column or easily repositioned into a horizontal position. Some models have a centre column that can be removed and positioned horizontally. Nevertheless, all tripods are significantly harder to manage than a simple copy stand.

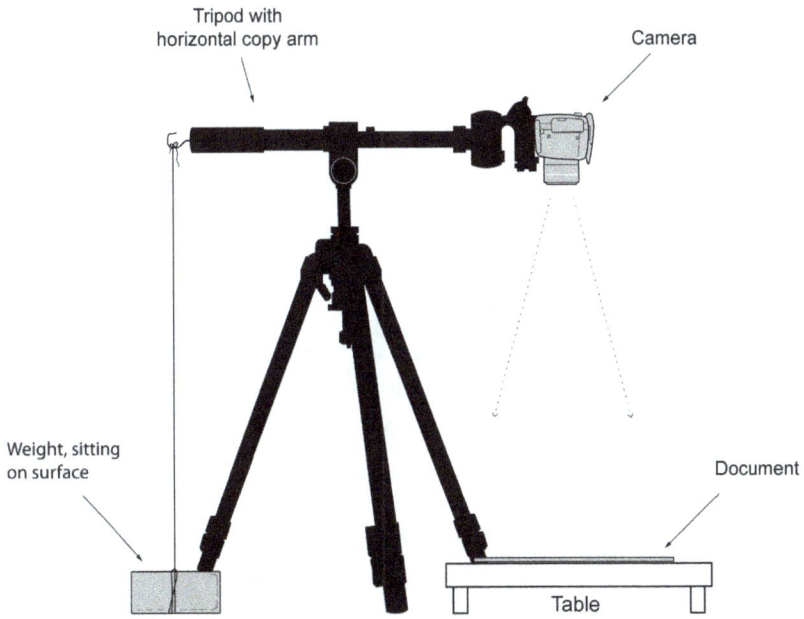

Figure 20. Tripod with horizontal copy arm.
Illustration © Anne Leaver, CC BY 4.0.

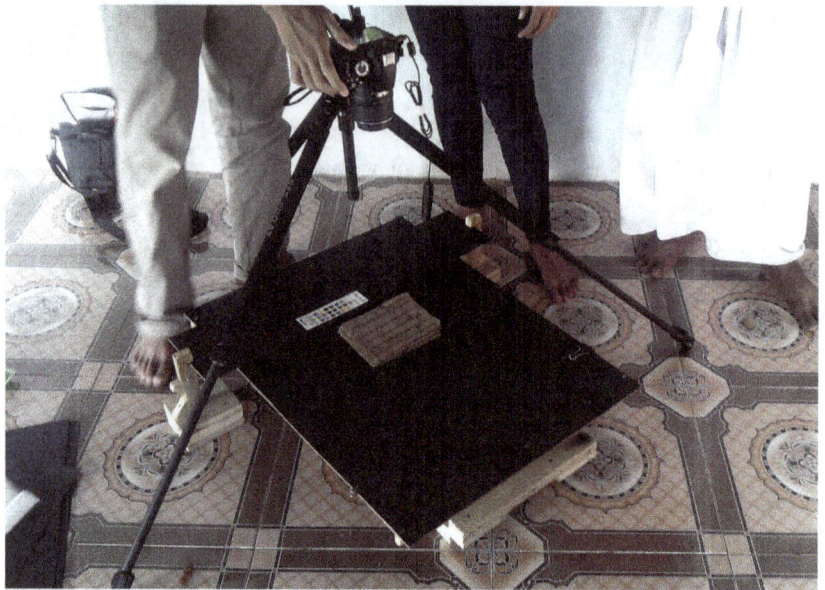

Figure 21. EAP698, Digitising Cham manuscripts in Vietnam. Here, a tripod and a portable platform are being used so that the manuscripts are not digitised on the ground. Photo © Hao Phan, CC BY 4.0.

Copy stand or tripod?

Advantages of copy stands
- Designed specifically for copying.
- Easy to set up with the camera properly squared up.
- More stable and rigid than a tripod.

Disadvantages of copy stands
- Most copy stands are not very portable.

Advantages of tripods
- A portable camera support that is easily transported and can be set up to photograph small and large items.
- Good for projects copying in multiple remote locations.

Disadvantages of tripods
- Harder to set up with the camera square.
- Awkward to use or unstable when copying with the camera pointing downwards.

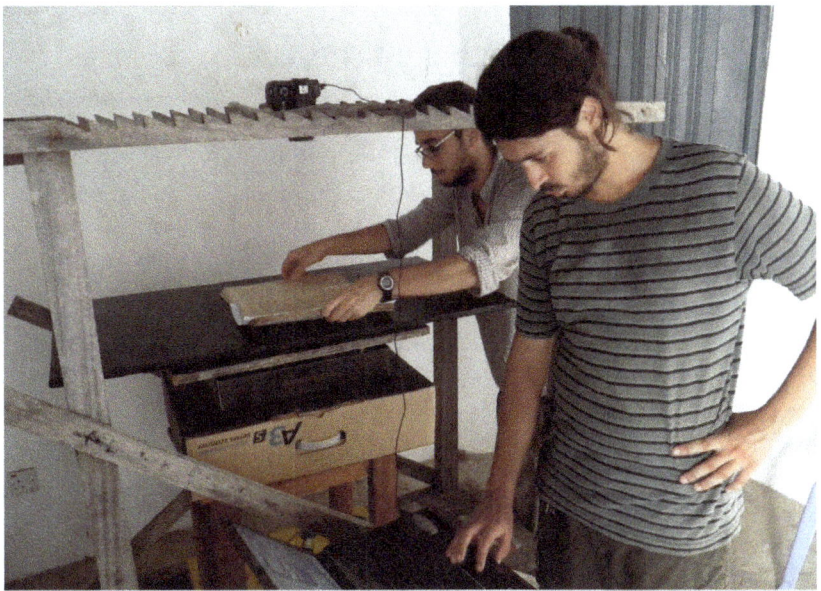

Figure 22. Finding a solution when your copy stand breaks: EAP569, Using a weaving loom to digitise Nzema cultural material from Ghana. Photo © Samuel Nobah, CC BY 4.0.

Lighting and flash

Working with continuous lighting

Some modular copy stands are available with lighting kits. These lights can be attached to the baseboard and positioned at different distances and angles, which helps prevent reflections from shiny surfaces. The best lights are LED or compact fluorescent tubes, which do not generate heat and will provide an even illumination across the frame, when carefully positioned. These lights are long-lasting (8000 hours) but it is probably worth taking spares in case the bulbs are damaged in transit or fail partway through the project. It is essential that all the lights being used are of precisely the same variety as otherwise a replacement bulb may well produce different coloured illumination and introduce colour casts.

If you are photographing objects larger than A3, then a copy stand with attached lighting may not be adequate. In this case, use lights which are separated from the baseboard.

Which light source?

Advantages of available light
- Daylight offers a free light source independent of electricity.
- Available light sources offer continuous light that is always visible (unlike flash), so surface reflections can be seen through the camera and controlled.

Disadvantages of available light
- The colour temperature of available light varies significantly.
- Care has to be taken with possible mixed lighting sources.
- Working outdoors potentially exposes archive material to dust, rain, wind and sunlight.

Advantages of electric lights
- A continuous light source that is always visible (unlike flash), so surface reflections can be seen through the camera and controlled.
- Dedicated LED lighting kits are available for some copy stands.

Disadvantages of electric lights
- Care has to be taken with possible mixed lighting sources.
- Lights are dependent on an electricity supply.
- Bright non-LED lights can get very hot.

Advantages of flash

Once mastered, a twin flash copy set-up offers:
- A very bright light source.
- Very sharp images with less risk of visible camera shake.
- A relatively portable lighting kit.
- No dependency on electricity (unless using rechargeable batteries).
- Flash overrides available light and eliminates most colour temperature problems from mixed lighting sources.

Disadvantages of flash
- Complex to set up and master.
- Expensive technology.
- Dependent on batteries.

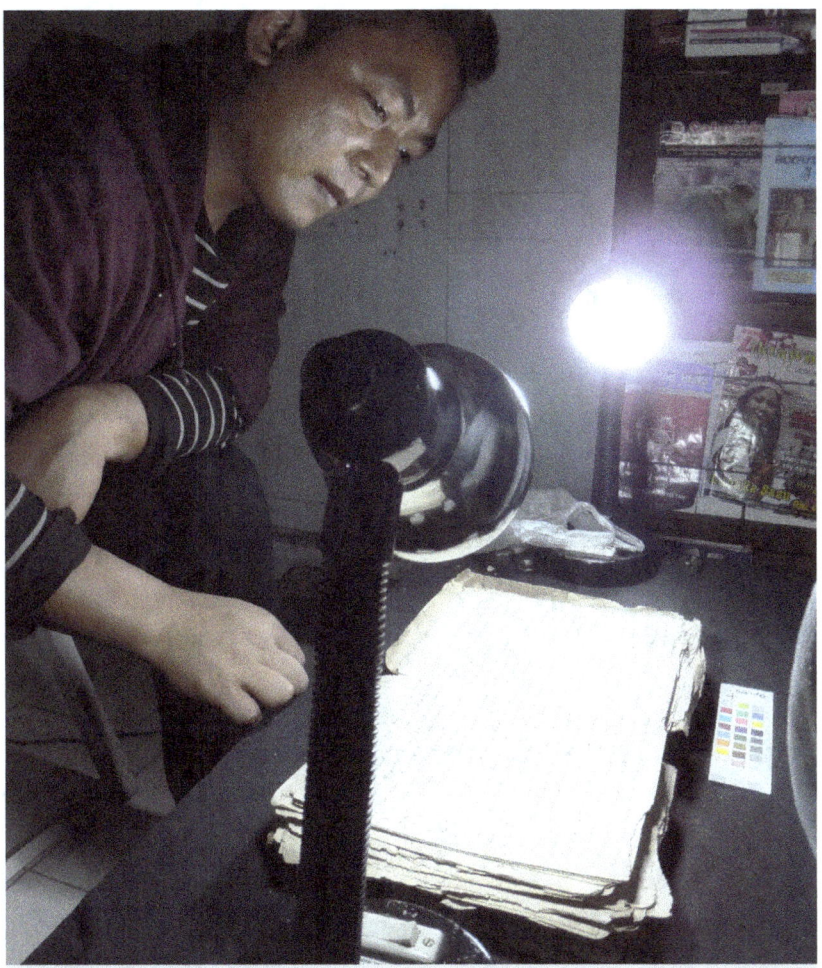

Figure 23. EAP454, Relying on basic desk lamps as the field workers move around the remote area of Mizoram, India.
Photo © Kyle Jackson, CC BY 4.0.

Flash photography

Electronic flash adds another level of complexity to the copying process and also adds significantly to the process of learning the camera controls. For that reason, the Endangered Archive Programme does not recommend using flash to researchers with little working knowledge of digital photography. However, electronic flash has some clear

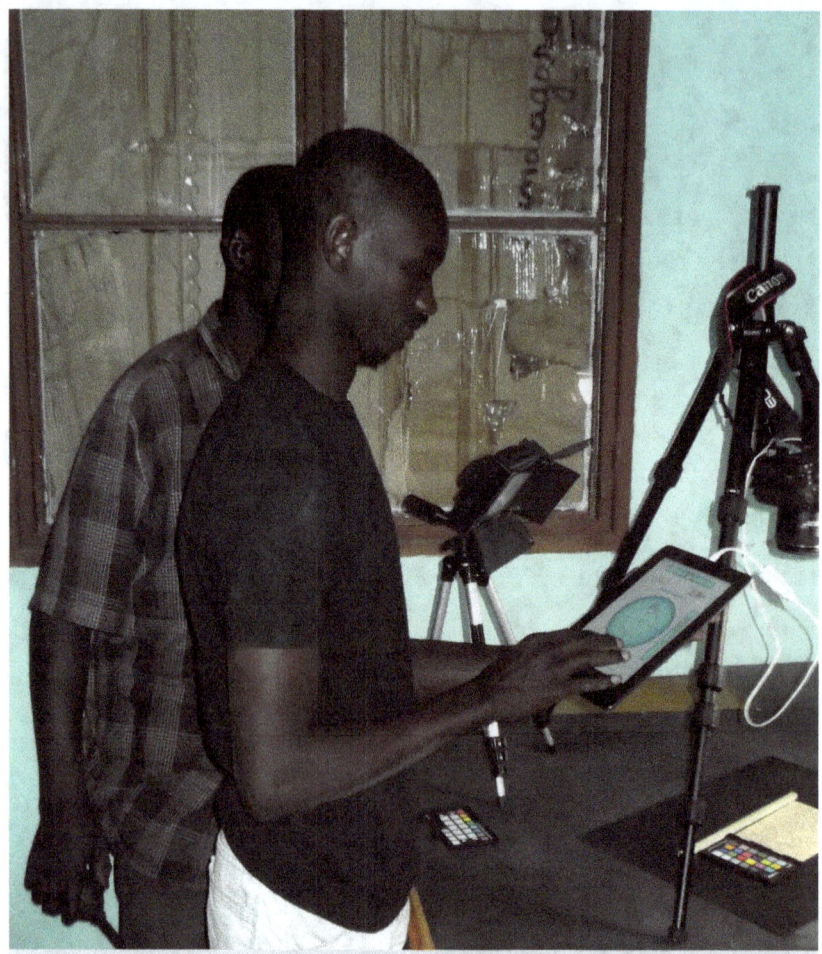

Figure 24. EAP764, Blocking out sunlight when digitising material from Bandiagara, Mali. Photo © Fabrizio Magnani, CC BY 4.0.

advantages, offering a very bright and repeatable light source that can speed up the copying process and remove the risk of camera shake caused by long exposures.

Some DSLR cameras have a small built-in flashgun, but **this should never be used when copying** as it will give very harsh and uneven results, especially at close working distances, and is likely to cause reflections from surfaces.

The ideal flash set-up for copying consists of two flashguns positioned equidistant from the material being copied and bounced off white reflectors, usually umbrellas. The umbrellas should be located on either side of the camera and pointed at the copying surface at an angle of about 45 degrees. Position the umbrellas far enough apart so that no part of the umbrella is directly above the material being copied.

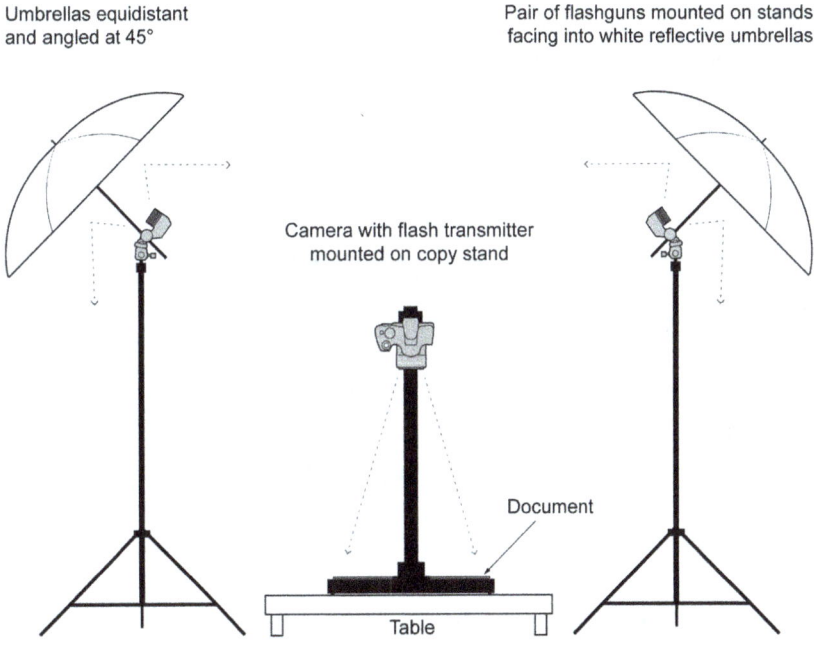

Figure 25. Drawn illustration showing the flashgun/umbrella set-up angled at 45 degrees to the copy surface.
Illustration © Anne Leaver, CC BY 4.0.

Flashguns will need to be mounted on stands fitted with a lighting head that holds both the flashgun and the umbrella. The flashguns point into the umbrella so that this wide white surface becomes the source of illumination for the material being copied.

(N.B. If photographing outdoors, when the umbrella is unfolded, lighting stands are very susceptible to being blown over by wind.)

Despite the additional learning necessary, such a flash kit has several very particular advantages. Battery-powered flashguns are portable and not directly dependent on electricity. Bounced flash offers a very bright, diffused and even illumination that produces very sharp images because flash provides a very brief burst of light. In most indoor situations away from direct sunlight, flash overrides other sources of local illumination, thus avoiding problems with mixed lighting sources (though it is still good policy to turn off indoor lights).

To read more about this see the Digital Appendix 2 at https://doi.org/10.11647/OBP.0138.11

Copying glass plate negatives and transparencies

Most copying with scanners or digital cameras uses the light reflected from the surface of objects like paper documents. But some objects like glass plate negatives or other transparent materials need a system for recording the light transmitted *through* the object. Such items can be scanned using the film rather than reflective setting on a flatbed scanner or photographed on a light box.

If you have a large number of transparencies or slides to copy you should purchase a dedicated film scanner, which will scan both negatives and positives. Film scanners are available in various formats.

If you are copying a significant amount of material like this, you will need to plan for the largest such items and choose a scanner or light box that is big enough to cope with the largest item. Scanners and most light boxes will need a reliable electricity supply.

When photographing glass plate negatives on a lightbox it is best to copy in near darkness, so that the only light source is the light transmitted, otherwise the camera may record surface reflections from the glass itself. It is also useful to mask off the area around the glass plate to avoid flare. If you are copying a large number of glass plates, then two L-shaped pieces of black card will simplify the masking process.

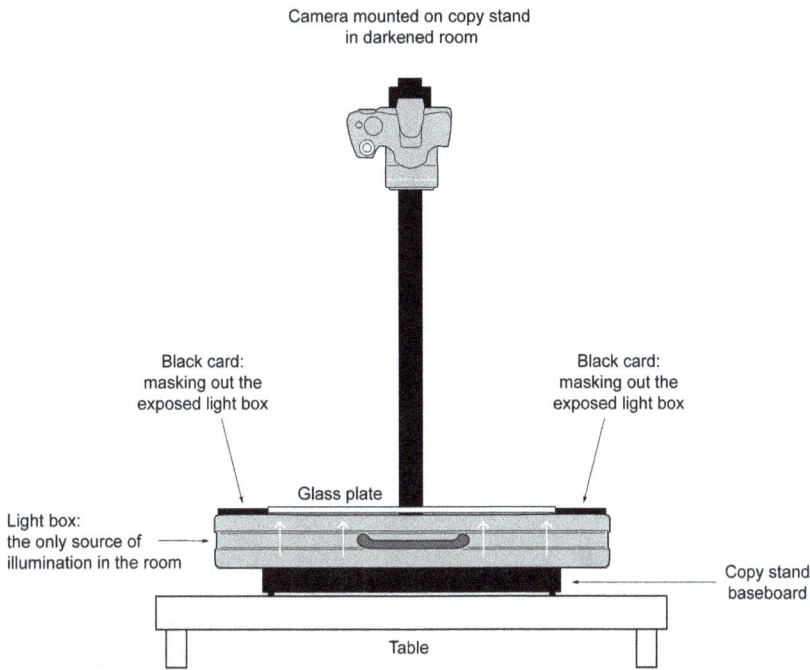

Figure 26. **Equipment set-up for digitising glass plate negatives using a copy stand and a light box.** Illustration © Anne Leaver, CC BY 4.0.

Photographic equipment for the field

An APS format camera kit

- An APS digital camera, macro lens and wide-angle to standard zoom lens with close focussing or macro capability.
- UV protection filters for all lenses.
- Spare camera batteries (at least one).
- Spare charger (a good idea if electricity is unreliable).
- A spare camera body (a duplicate of the chosen camera or perhaps a cheaper APS camera) for larger projects.
- A remote control to fit the specific camera model.

A full-frame camera kit
- A full-frame digital camera and 50mm standard lens or macro lens.
- A wide-angle to standard zoom lens with close focussing or macro capability.
- UV protection filters for all lenses.
- Spare camera batteries (at least one).
- Spare charger (a good idea if electricity is unreliable).
- A spare camera body (a duplicate of the chosen camera or perhaps a cheaper full-frame camera) for larger projects.
- A remote control to fit the specific camera model.

A copying kit
- A copy stand.
- Alternatively, a tripod and lateral arm/tripod with convertible centre column.
- LED lights or a portable flash set-up.
- Background cloth or card of neutral colour (plus gaffer tape to hold cloth flat and in place).
- Colour checker and measure.
- A small spirit level.

Data storage
- Spare high-quality and fast memory cards (CF or SD or both depending on the camera model chosen).
- CF or SD card reader for the above.
- Two external hard drives to back up data.

A portable flash kit
- Two portable lighting stands.
- Two adjustable brackets to fit the flashgun and umbrella to the stands.
- Two white umbrella reflectors.
- Two flashguns.
- One optical transmitter.
- Spare sets of disposable lithium batteries or good quality rechargeable batteries if electricity supplies are reliable.

Other
- Full notes on equipment and documentation procedures.
- A bulb-style air blower, microfibre cloth for cleaning camera bodies, and lens tissues for cleaning lenses.

Essential equipment and skills

Digital cameras and flashguns have become extremely complex pieces of equipment. They and the manuals that accompany them can seem quite intimidating at first, but in fact, they contain far more information than you need to absorb to work effectively. **However, it is absolutely essential that you purchase and get to know your equipment well in advance of taking it into the field.** This may well take several days of practice and experimentation. Make notes of the key settings for camera and flashguns and take these with you into the field.

It is probably worth the small extra cost of buying equipment from a good local camera store, if that is possible, and benefitting from technical support from knowledgeable staff.

Essential skills for the digital camera

To be competent and confident, you must know how to:
- Turn the camera on and off, adjust the zoom, focus the lens, take photographs and view them on the rear LED screen.
- Attach and remove a lens.
- Set the exposure mode to Aperture Priority or Manual exposure. Change the lens from auto focussing to manual focussing.
- Adjust the aperture, the shutter speed and the ISO setting.
- Set the auto white balance.
- Use the exposure compensation control when using Aperture Priority exposure mode.
- Set the correct exposure when using Manual exposure mode.
- Turn on the electronic grid in the viewfinder (or replace the focussing screen with a gridded screen).
- Turn on the rear LED screen and adjust settings displayed on the screen (aperture, shutter speed, ISO, auto white balance).
- View histograms on the rear LED screen.
- Set the camera to record in RAW.
- Remove, recharge and replace batteries.
- Remove and replace memory cards.
- Download the files from memory cards onto a computer and back up files from the computer to an external hard drive.
- Reformat memory cards within the camera.

Counterfeit goods

There is a burgeoning international market in counterfeit digital goods. This is particularly common for peripherals like camera batteries and memory cards. Counterfeit camera batteries could potentially damage the camera or constitute a fire hazard. Counterfeit memory cards are also common and threaten the correct writing of files and long term reliable storage and retrieval of data.

Important: It is essential to purchase all digital peripherals from reliable sources. For example, we would recommend using genuine Nikon batteries in Nikon cameras and genuine Canon batteries in Canon cameras.

Practical advice for photography in the field

Electricity supplies and battery power in the field

If you are working in remote locations where electricity is unreliable, you will need spare camera batteries. Depending on the scale of the documentation being undertaken and the number of files being generated, you might need several extra camera batteries and perhaps should plan for spare charging systems. You will also need to check the availability of power supplies for recharging and the commonest local type of electrical socket. In remote conditions, electricity supplies can be very variable and recharging batteries and laptops to full capacity can be slow. For a large project you might consider a small portable generator and/or high quality solar chargers. In situations with variable electricity supplies, it is essential to invest in a heavy-duty surge protector to protect electronic equipment from damage.

Lithium batteries

Digital cameras, video cameras and many other electronic devices use rechargeable lithium batteries. N.B. Most airlines now insist that all spare or loose lithium batteries are carried in hand luggage (that is, unless they are inside the camera body).

Disposable lithium batteries are expensive, but are the best-quality batteries in terms of both power and shelf life. They also work well in extreme cold, continuing to function down to minus 40°C. Most conventional disposable alkaline batteries and rechargeable NiMH batteries lose power significantly when used below freezing point.

Altitude and hard drives

Conventional hard drives are the most common computer storage medium, used in laptops and external hard drives. They are spinning disks, which are at risk when working at altitudes above 10,000 feet. In extreme conditions, hard drives can be destroyed by being moved around at high altitude. In contrast, solid state drives (SSDs) have no moving parts and are unaffected by altitude. SSDs are available for use as internal drives for laptops or desktops and as external drives. They are significantly more expensive than conventional drives. If you are using conventional hard drives at altitude, it is essential that you turn off the computer prior to moving it, rather than putting it into sleep mode, or disconnect and turn off the external hard drive. **Do not travel at high altitude with a laptop in sleep mode.**

Care of photographic equipment

Modern semi-professional digital cameras are rugged and reliable pieces of equipment, with very good moisture and dust seals. They are therefore more suitable for surviving the rigours of fieldwork than cheaper models. However, all digital cameras are susceptible to problems caused by dust and moisture. You should avoid exposing the camera, lenses, batteries and flashguns to water, to high humidity and to dust. Store and ship cameras with dessicant pouches (e.g. silica gel) inside sealed watertight containers if working in humid conditions and dry these pouches regularly. Try to avoid changing the camera lens outside and **never** leave the camera without a lens or body cap attached. Always protect the camera and lenses when travelling.

Cleaning dust off cameras and lenses

When you change lenses, dust can enter the camera body and land on the filter in front of the sensor. This results in visible blotches that occur in the same place on every frame. They are most noticeable in large areas of lighter tones. Most cameras clean the sensor automatically when they are turned on or off. They do this by vibrating the sensor so that dust particles fall off, though there are times when dust specks are not removed by this process.

N.B. Dust on the sensor is only noticeable after you have taken a photograph and are reviewing it on the rear LCD or on a computer screen. Particles of dust that are visible in the viewfinder are either on the viewfinder or on the mirror inside the camera body. Such dust does not appear on the image and if distracting can be removed easily by a quick blast from a rubber bulb-style blower.

- Use a blower and then gentle wipes with a lint-free, clean, soft microfibre cloth to clean the camera body, viewfinder and LCD screens. Only use proprietary lens tissues to clean optical surfaces.
- Use a blower to clean the mirror: remove the lens and hold the camera facing downwards so that dust particles can fall out of the body. Give several puffs of air to the mirror from a blower. Take great care not to touch the mirror. Never use a compressed air can.

Cleaning dust off sensors

Cleaning the sensor properly is a job for a professional service centre. You can render the warranty of a camera void by attempting to clean the sensor yourself. It is also very easy to damage a sensor by touching it and they are extremely expensive to replace.

However, in circumstances where there is dust on the sensor and the automated cleaning process is not working and there is no alternative, you can try the following:

- Switch the camera to manual sensor cleaning, which will lock up the mirror and open the shutter. Remove the lens, which will allow you to see the sensor, and then hold the camera facing downwards so that the dust particles can fall out of the body. Give several puffs of air to the sensor from a blower. Keep the tip of the blower just inside the camera and well away from the sensor. Under no circumstances touch the sensor. Do NOT use compressed air. Replace the lens, turn the camera off and then on again and take test shots to see if the dust has cleared.
- To check for dust on the sensor: choose Aperture Priority (A on a Nikon, Av on a Canon) and set the lens to f16. Fill the frame with a

clean white sheet of paper or a similar single pale tone, focus and shoot. Examine the file on a computer screen. Repeat if necessary.

Packing equipment for travel

Camera bags are available in a bewildering variety, from rigid metal boxes offering the maximum protection for photographic equipment, roller bags offering the easiest form of transportation (provided you are not working off-road), to backpacks that offer ergonomic solutions to carrying weight. It is recommended that you purchase the bag after you have purchased the rest of the equipment and take into consideration the nature of the environment in which you will be working. The choice will depend on the amount of equipment you are carrying, and whether you will be working in a single archival institution or travelling. Even if you are working in a single archive, some kind of camera bag would be advisable for storing equipment and keeping it all in one place.

Although professional equipment is tough and reliable, it is quite susceptible to damage in transport. Good quality sealable plastic food bags are excellent for keeping dust off equipment. Bubble wrap is a lightweight solution to protect equipment in transit. Good quality sealable plastic food boxes can protect equipment from water and knocks.

What to put in the aircraft hold

If you are flying with equipment rather than purchasing it locally or shipping it separately, there are limitations to what you can carry in hand luggage.

Small items of equipment can be placed into sealable polythene bags, wrapped in bubble wrap, and then placed inside good quality waterproof sealable plastic food boxes and surrounded by clothing in luggage checked into the hold. Tripod and lighting stands benefit from being well wrapped in bubble wrap and carried in tripod bags.

Camera bodies, lenses and laptops are best carried in hand luggage, again individually placed into sealable polythene bags, wrapped in bubble wrap and then inside good quality waterproof sealable plastic food boxes or soft padded cases within a camera bag.

Hard drives and data management

Choice of external hard drive

Given the vulnerability of digital data when working in remote locations, it is probably worth investing in SSD (Solid State Drive) models for reasons of speed, overall reliability and the reduced risk of internal physical damage to moving parts. It is essential to check for compatibility with project computers when purchasing separate hard drives: external drives are available with a variety of different connection ports but USB 3.0 is common and works on Macs and PCs. Many external drives are bus powered, meaning that they do not need a separate AC supply but are powered directly by the computer through the connecting lead. This may be essential in some remote conditions. Other models have a separate AC supply and lead.

Managing digital files while in the field

It is very easy to delete original digital files by accident. It is recommended that, while in the field, you never delete files from the memory card. Only delete original files when you are certain that all the files have been checked and backed up.

When reusing memory cards, it is best practice to reformat cards within the camera rather than just emptying them by dragging the files off the card and into the computer waste bin. Reformatting memory cards helps ensure against folder and file corruption. Regular reformatting is good practice and should eliminate potential card errors. Never use a card that has displayed an error reading.

> **Reformatting destroys all the existing files and folders on the memory card.** Make certain you have downloaded and backed up all the files in two or three different locations beforehand.
>
> (For a detailed discussion of backing up data, see Chapter 5.)

Hard drive and flash memory card capacity

A full-frame digital camera like the Canon 5D Mark II will generate RAW files of approximately 30 Mb (30 megabytes) or more. A 32 Gb (32 gigabyte) Compact Flash card or SD card will hold more than 1000 such RAW files while a 500 Gb (500 gigabyte) hard drive will hold more than 16,000 such files. Hard drives are a relatively inexpensive part of the overall budget, so always overestimate your digital storage needs.

Formatting hard drives for submission of material

Hard drives for PCs and Macs are not necessarily interchangeable. Researchers working with Apple Macintosh computers will have to reformat the external hard drive they submit to the British Library as exFAT or FAT32. This makes them readable on both Mac and PC. The FAT32 format does have some limitations, as it imposes an individual file size limit of 4GB. The exFAT format does not have this limitation. Drives submitted to the British Library should always be unpartitioned and never password protected. You can reformat hard drives on an Apple Mac via the Disk Utility software found in the Utilities folder, within the Applications folder that comes preinstalled on all Macs.

Scanners

It may be felt that a flatbed scanner is the most appropriate equipment for your project, but do not be misled into thinking it is an easier option than a camera. The advantages mean that there is less potential for distortion when using a flatbed scanner and it is simpler to align the document. Scanners also export images in TIFF format which means you do not have to convert from RAW. However, the documents must be of a certain size and you need to have a reliable electricity supply if you wish to consider using a scanner.

Flatbed scanners have improved significantly, and they can produce excellent images. The information that manufacturers supply can be baffling, making the task of deciding which model to choose rather bewildering. The information below will hopefully help you with the various specifications and what to look for.

Resolution

Manufacturers can specify two types of resolution: optical or interpolated. You should only be interested in the optical figures which give you the best indication of how a scanner will perform. Optical resolution is shown in the format of two figures referring to samples per inch (for example 1200 x 2400 dpi). It is the first figure, which is the smaller of the two, that is the most important number. Ideally, it should not be below 1200 dpi.[5]

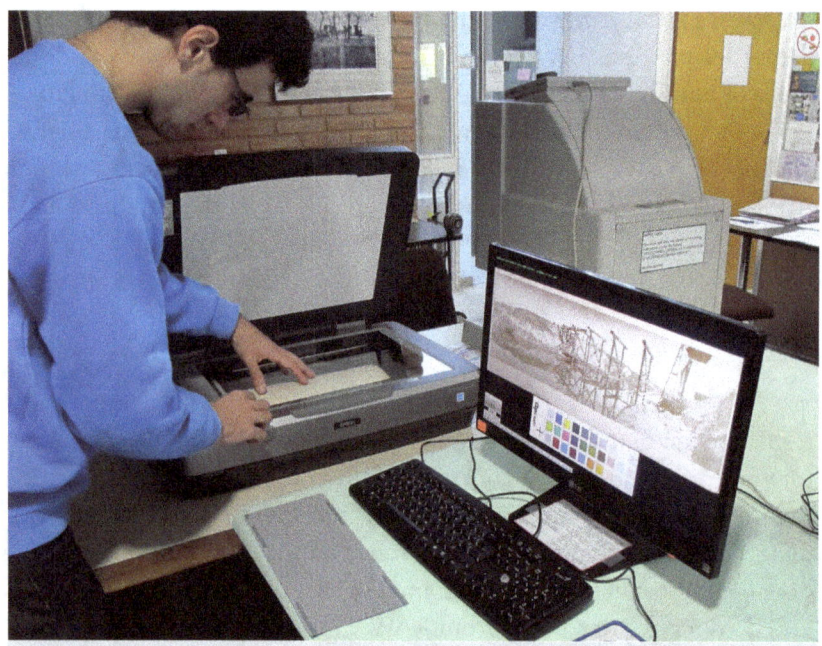

Figure 27. EAP563, Scanning photographs from the Hume family collection, Argentina. Photo © Silvana Lucia Piga, CC BY 4.0.

---

5   You may also see 'spi' or 'ppi', but they all describe the same resolution.

Colour depth

This may be referred to as colour depth or bit depth. It indicates how well the equipment can capture the colour range: the higher the number, the more accurate the colour. Scanners may capture at a higher bit depth but sometimes are only able to export at a lower depth; it is therefore important to understand the colour depth that the scanner will export and ignore the figure a scanner can capture. Colour is made up of three different channels: red, green and blue (RGB). The colour depth will either reflect each of the channels, in which case it will be given as 8- or 16-bit/channel, or it will combine all the channels and be shown as 24- or 48-bit RGB. The more accurate the colour, the bigger the image size and the more storage you will need. Usually for EAP projects, the recommendation is 8-bit/channel (24-bit RGB).

Noise

Noise is any unwanted energy that interferes with the image you wish to produce. Often this will be apparent by a grainy appearance, particularly in the shadow. To understand how much noise might be created, you need to look at the signal to noise (s/n) ratio that will be quoted on the scanner specification. Lower end scanners with an unacceptable ratio may not even quote this figure — this sort of scanner is to be avoided. Acceptable levels would be 60 dB for 8-bit/channel and 75 dB for 12-bit.

If you know the colour depth and the s/n ratio, you can start making informed decisions about which scanner to buy. A scanner with a high signal to noise ratio with 30-bit colour depth will outperform a scanner with a lower s/n ratio at 42-bit.

Dynamic range and dMax

Another specification that you should consider when purchasing a scanner is the dynamic range. This is the difference between the brightest highlight and the darkest shadow. This would be particularly relevant if you are considering a scanner to digitise black and white photography. The optimum scale has white (dMin) at 0.0 and the darkest black (dMax) at 4.0. Scanners cannot capture at these extremes but if a model claims to have a dMin of 0.2 and a dMax of 3.8, the dynamic range will be 3.6. The lower the dynamic range, the less likely the scanner will be able to reproduce the subtleties of shading and greyscale. If the specification only quotes the dMax figure, you want it to be as close to 4.0 as possible.

Scanning speed

When choosing a scanner, it is important to find out how long it takes to scan a document. Of course, the higher the quality of image, the longer the scan will take. If at all possible, ask for a demonstration before you purchase anything. If there are two models with very similar standards, the scanning speed may help you make your final choice.

Scan area

It is vital that you know the full extent of the dimensions of the material that you will be digitising. The most common size for a flatbed scanner is A4. A3 scanners are on the market, but anything larger is extremely expensive. There are also specific scanners that digitise film, such as transparencies, slides or 35mm film. As this sort of material would not normally fall within an EAP project, we have not covered this type of scanner. It is important, however, to mention that it is easy to break glass plate negatives when closing the lid of a scanner, so it is preferable to use a lightbox. If you do decide to use a scanner for glass negatives, please refer to page 78.

If you do not know the dimensions of the documents you are digitising, choose a camera and copy stand set-up rather than a scanner.

Colour management

It is important to calibrate the scanner and make sure that the colours are as true a representation as possible. Often scanners have built-in methods of calibration. An additional method is to use a colour checker and accompanying software. The chart uses precise colour and grey values and allows the scanner to make appropriate adjustments. It is important to calibrate the scanner on a regular basis (ideally on a daily basis or at the very least once a week); this way you know your images will be consistent throughout your digitisation project.

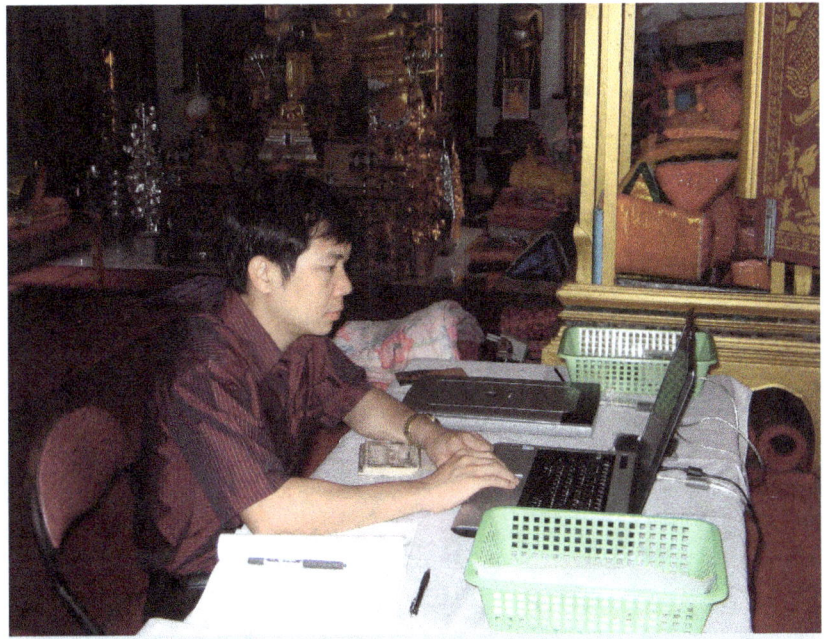

Figure 28. EAP086, A temporary scanning set-up while digitising photographs in a monastery in Laos.
This highlights the methodical process required no matter where you are. Photo © Martin Jürgens, CC BY 4.0.

3. Image standards

Elizabeth Hunter

Introduction

The most important aspect of digitising a manuscript is to make sure that the text is in focus and legible. There are, however, other factors you should consider to ensure your images are as pleasing to the eye as possible. If you are new to photography, this is a skill you will need to develop. For some people it will come naturally; for others it will take a little more time to learn. To help improve your judgement of what makes a good photograph, we have included several examples of digitised items; some of them are perfect, whilst others show varying levels of inadequacy. Look closely at the examples to understand what constitutes a high-quality image.

When you are awarded your grant, you will need to send sample images to the EAP curator for approval. It is important to send your samples as soon as you start digitising. The temptation can be to digitise many items before you decide to submit them. The risk in doing this is that they may not meet the appropriate standards, and this can result in low morale if you are told that they are not quite right. The material you are digitising is fragile and vulnerable and you only want to handle it once, so getting it right first time is important. It is wise to spend time familiarising yourself with the equipment and assessing the quality of the photographs you are producing. Compare your photographs with the examples provided in this chapter; this should help you decide whether you are on the right track.

© Elizabeth Hunter, CC BY 4.0   https://doi.org/10.11647/OBP.0138.03

Digitising to the highest standard is essential. It is highly possible that there will never be a second chance to access these endangered materials.

Jian Xu, EAP012, EAP081, EAP143, EAP217, EAP460 and EAP550, China

The photographing of the manuscripts used only natural light and this presented a challenge on overcast or rainy days. On such days, the team had to wait until lighting conditions improved or even had to cancel the appointments with the manuscript owners. This not only delayed the work but also wasted time of the manuscripts' owners who are busy farmers.

Hao Phan, EAP698, Vietnam

Most of the times our work depended on the climate of Assam. Once the rainy season started we had to stop our work as the photographing of the manuscripts had to be done outdoors to get proper light. Indoor photography was generally impossible because the mud houses of most of the owners were poorly lit. Also the incessant rain made it difficult to move around. The rainy season generally runs for about half the year.

Stephen Morey and Poppy Gogoi, EAP373, Assam

The museum was a long shed with windows along the whole length, so we blacked out the windows of a railway coach. To do this we had to scour the local shops for black cloth!

Tim Procter, EAP626, Sierra Leone

Considerations

Lighting

It is a good idea, if possible, to replicate the controlled conditions of a studio, by blocking out light from windows and using the light of your studio flash to illuminate the objects being photographed.

The output from the flash will generally overpower ambient light, but if you have strong sunlight, then it can affect your camera exposure, and you may find that your images are brighter on one side than the other.

If it is not possible to photograph inside, then a cloudy day will give a nice soft light. If you have strong sunlight, then a white sheet placed above your working area will make the sunshine much more diffused.

Your lights need to illuminate the object and not cause problems of their own — for example, flare or unevenness — so you should ensure the lights are placed at equal distance from the items being photographed, and preferably at an angle of 45 degrees.

The larger the softbox (a softbox is a large fabric-covered frame that is placed over the bulb to produce soft and even lighting) or the umbrella you use with your lights, the more diffused, soft and even the lighting will be.

Colour checkers and white balance

You should ensure the computer and cameras are calibrated and that the cameras are 'white balanced' so that what is viewed on your computer screen is an accurate example of what has been captured.

You should begin your day's work by photographing a control shot with a colour checker target on a plain white background.

Comparing these control shot images will highlight any shift in colour balance and exposure, and the plain white background will show up any dust or marks on the camera sensor.

You should always include an accurate colour checker (including measurement scale) in each of your images.

Background

It is advisable to use a neutral grey or black background, preferably nothing too shiny or with too much texture, something like thick paper, under the items being photographed. This will provide a clean, uniform surface, and give a tidy look to the images.

Framing

Aim to fill the frame with the item as much as possible, and put the greyscale and measurement scale in the blank area over to one side of the frame. You don't want to lose valuable image space by putting the scales in the wrong place.

It is a good idea to use a spirit level to get the camera parallel to the item being photographed, and try to make the item as flat and level as possible, by propping up any low parts with Plastazote and holding down any higher parts with a Perspex pointer.

When you are photographing a book that has many pages, make sure that the distance between the page being photographed and the camera remains the same, so the images are all the same size and all remain in focus as you work your way through the book. This will mean measuring the distance when you begin photographing and keeping a note of it, then remeasuring and readjusting the camera position every 20 pages or so.

This does depend on how thick the pages are; you may find you only need to move the camera closer, for instance, every 50 pages if the paper is thin. This is something that you will need to judge.

The measurement scale and the greyscale should remain level with the page being photographed, which will mean propping them up on pieces of foam or cardboard when you are at the beginning of your book and reducing these as you progress through the book.

Photographing negatives

If you need to digitise glass or gelatine negatives, then one of the best ways is by using a copy stand with a camera attached, and a lightbox below it (see Figure 26).

The negative is placed onto the lightbox and masked with black paper so that only the negative is illuminated. This will need a slow shutter speed, maybe around 1 second, because the total illumination is coming from the lightbox through the negative.

Table 3. EAP standards for digital material

From originals	
Black-and-white photographs	8-bit greyscale, resolution dependant on size of original, likely to be in the range 300–1200 ppi. It may be appropriate to capture as 24-bit RGB depending on image tone.
Colour photographs	24-bit RGB, resolution dependant on size of original likely to be in the range 300–1200 ppi.
Slides or small negatives	8-bit greyscale or 24-bit RGB, effective resolution of 300 ppi relative to the size of the original.
Printed texts	8-bit greyscale, 400 ppi.
Printed texts with half-tone, and other black-and-white illustrations	8-bit greyscale, 400 ppi, 24-bit RGB may be considered depending on characteristic of material.
Printed texts with colour illustrations	24-bit RGB, 400 ppi.
Manuscripts, maps and other materials	300 ppi, 8-bit greyscale or 24-bit RGB. Spatial resolution can be adjusted to 400 ppi and greater where significant elements to be captured are less than 1.5mm.

The EAP checking process

When you begin digitising, you must submit sample images to EAP for checking and approval. Do not begin digitising the archive until any comments have been addressed and approval is received.

Examples of good and bad images

Below are some examples pairing images that meet EAP guidelines and those that do not. Look at them carefully to notice the difference in each case.

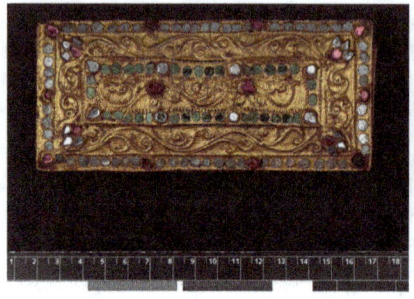 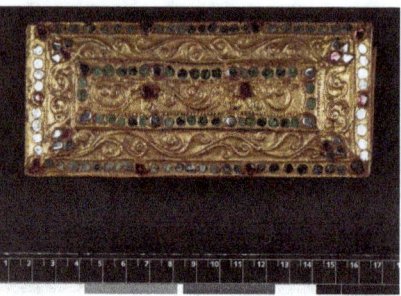

✓ The flare has been reduced by using a light tent or bouncing the light from the ceiling.   ✗ The surface has flare due to the light hitting it.

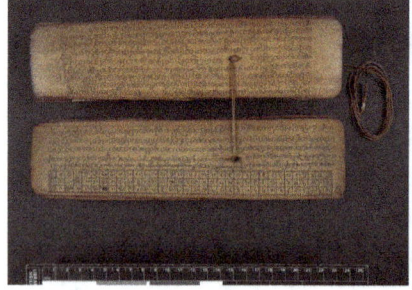 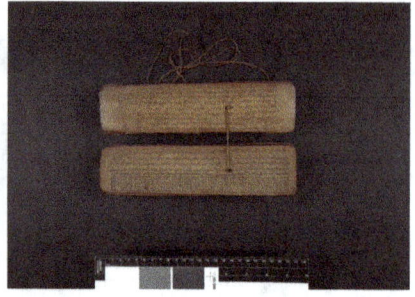

✓ The manuscript fills the frame of the photograph.   ✗ There is too much border around the item which has resulted in a lot of wastage of the frame.

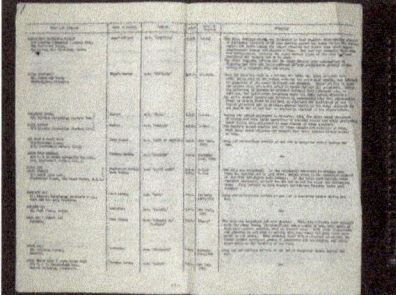 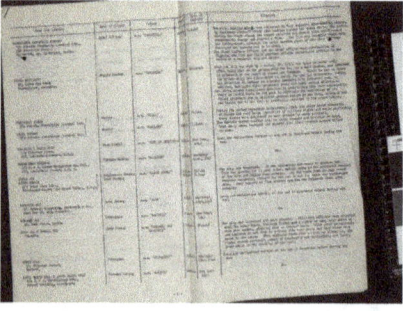

✓ The whole item is in the frame.   ✗ The edges of the item are not visible.

3. Image Standards

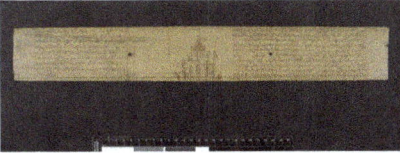

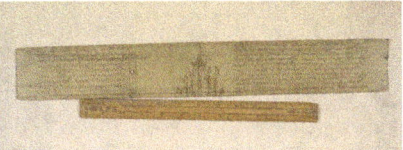

✓ The background colour is more suitable and the ruler placed neatly on the edge of the frame.

✗ The background is too similar in colour to the item; the item is not straight, and the ruler is too close.

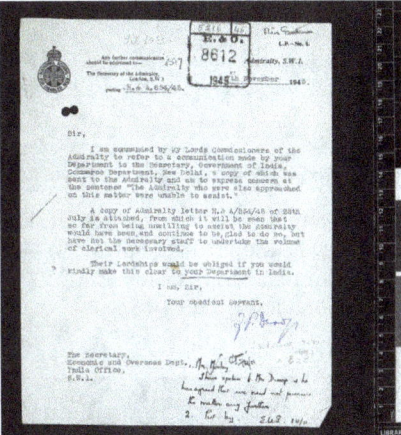

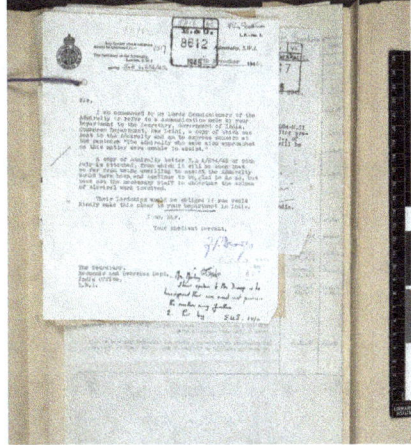

✓ A single item from an archival folder has been photographed. (This was possible due to an archival tag being used.)

✗ The entire stack of archival papers has been photographed. The papers underneath detract from the letter that is the focus of the photograph.

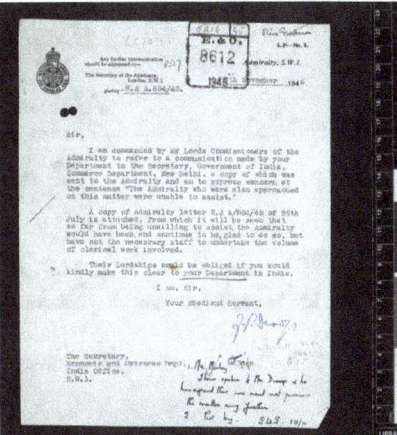

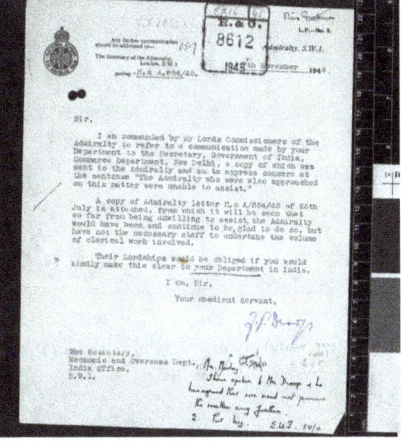

✓ The item is straight, and the ruler neatly on the edge of the frame.

✗ The item is not straight in the frame and the ruler is too close.

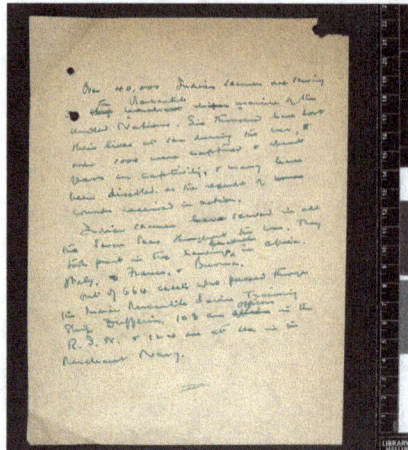 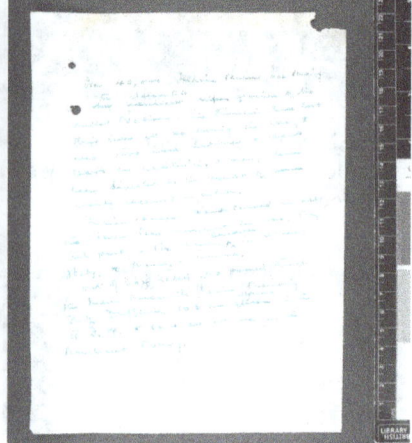

✓ The item has the correct exposure.

✗ The item is overexposed. Try either moving the lights further away, using a smaller f/stop, or a faster shutter speed, or a lower ISO setting.

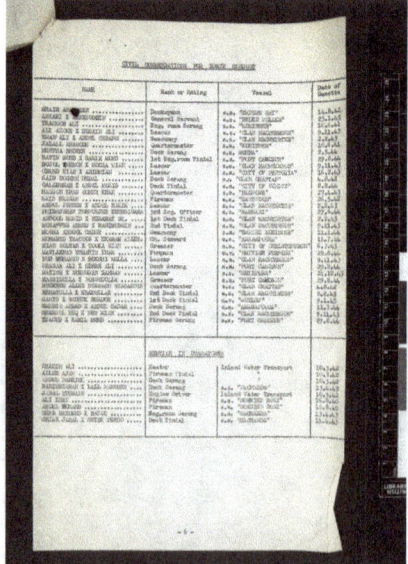 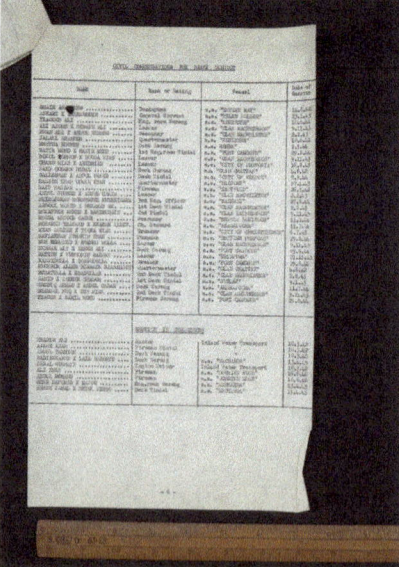

✓ The ruler occupies the empty space at the edge of the image.

✗ The ruler is in the wrong place, resulting in wasted space.

3. Image Standards

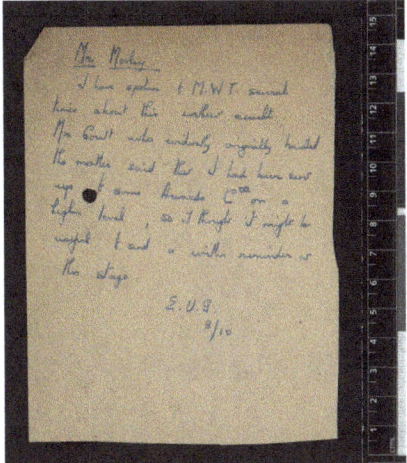 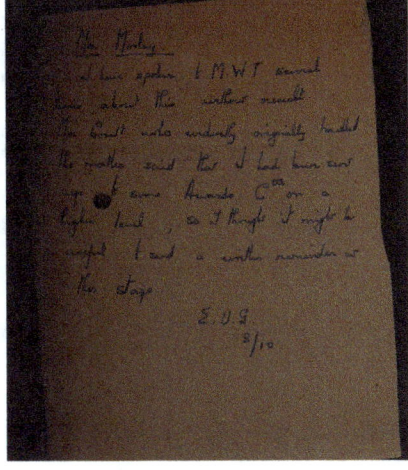

✓ The image has the correct exposure, straight in the frame, and has a ruler neatly on the edge.

✗ The image is too dark, not straight, and there is no ruler.

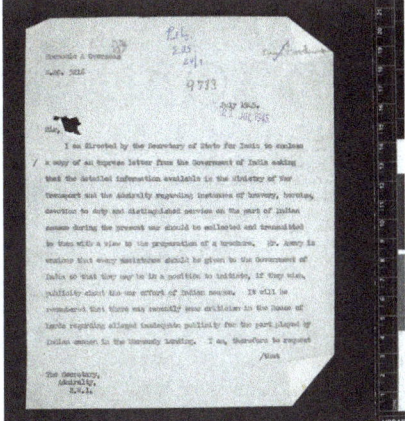 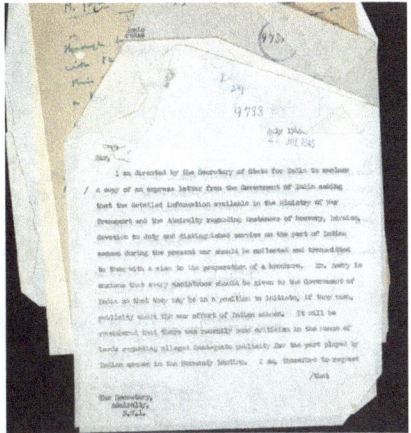

✓ The item is isolated from the others and has a ruler neatly on the side.

✗ The item is loose but has not been separated from the others, and there is no scale in the image.

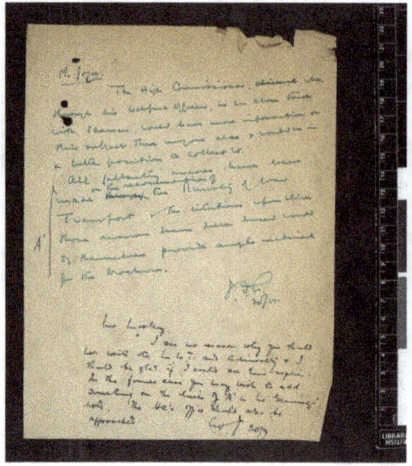

✓ The item fills the frame and the ruler is placed neatly on the side.

✗ The item is too small in the frame, and the ruler and colour checker take up too much space.

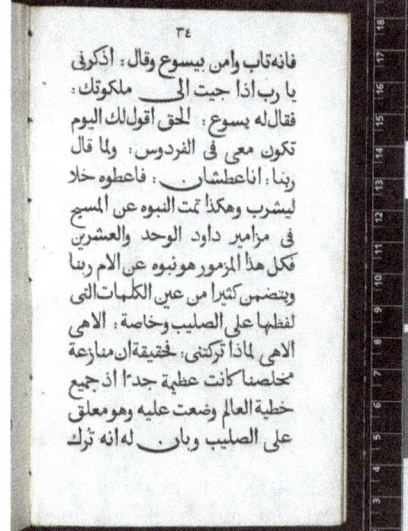
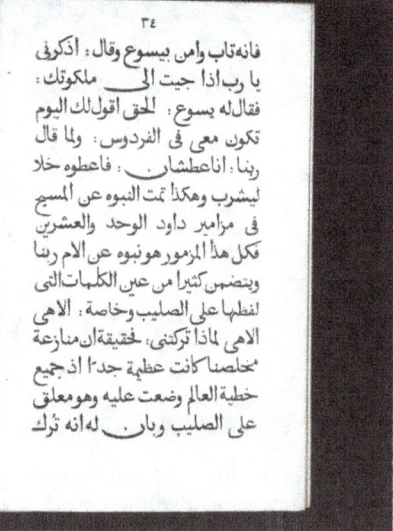

✓ The 'gutter' of the book is clearly visible and the scale is neatly on the side.

✗ The 'gutter' of the book is not in the frame, and there is no scale.

✓ The item fills the frame, and the scale is placed neatly on the side.

✗ The item is too small in the frame, and the scale and colour checker take up too much space.

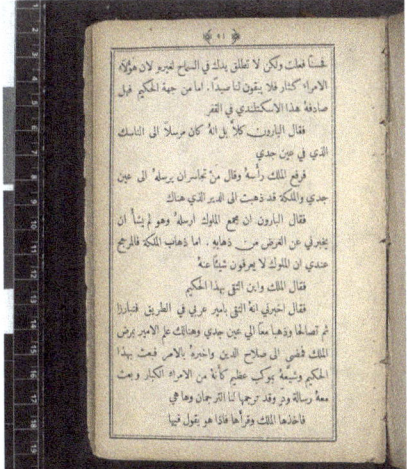
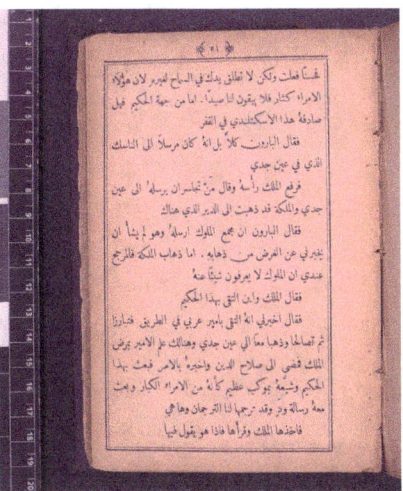

✓ The camera has been white balanced so the item appears with the correct colour.

✗ The camera has not been white balanced, so the item appears with the wrong colour.

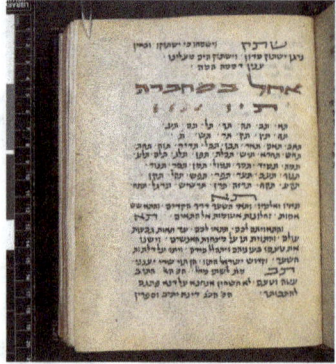 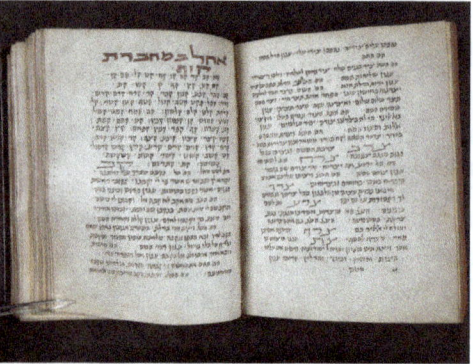

✓ The book has been opened to no more than 120 degrees, and one page fills the frame.

✗ The book has been opened too far, and cannot lie flat, so the two opposing pages are not level, resulting in distortion, 'gutter' shadow, and loss of focus.

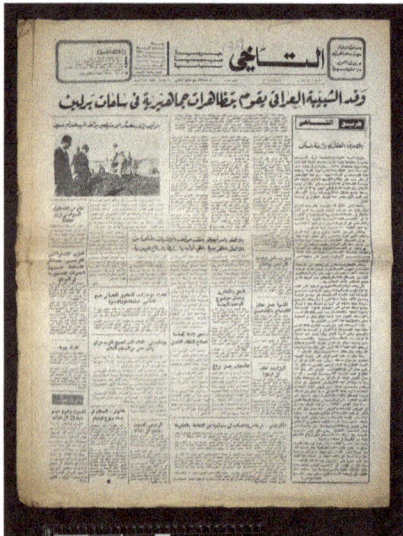 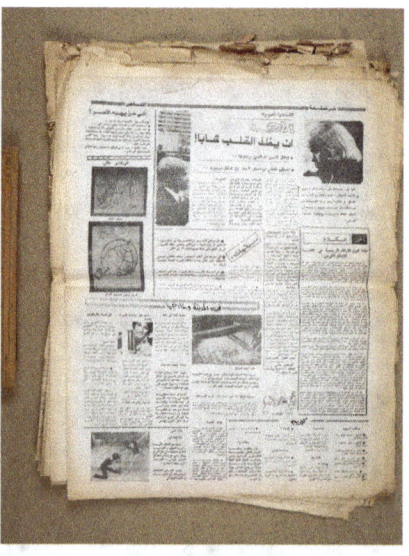

✓ The item is isolated on a black background and fills the frame.

✗ The item is on the wrong colour background, and is too small in the frame.

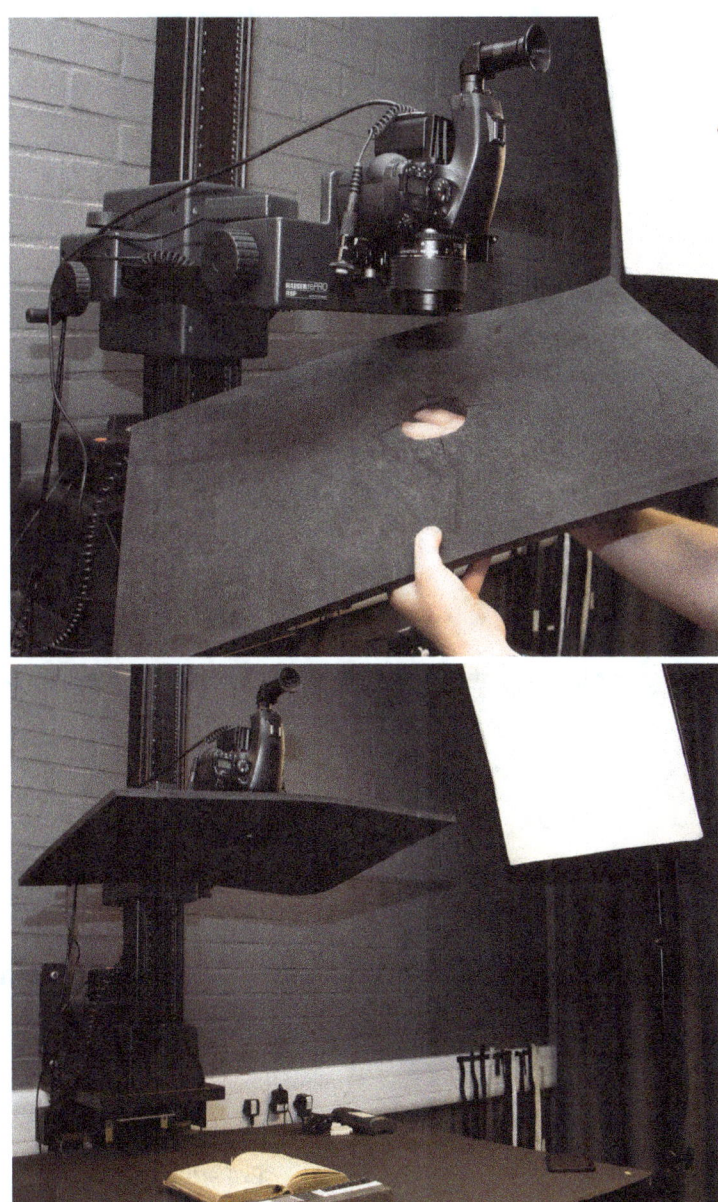

Figure 29. Preventing light appearing in an image.
Using a thin sheet of foam, attached to the camera lens, will prevent the light source appearing in the image (in this case the lamp). Photos © Elizabeth Hunter, CC BY 4.0.

Techniques to prevent common problems

Sometimes the reflection from the lamps and light sources can appear in the photograph. To avoid this, you can place black card or Plastazote over the lens as shown below.

When you are digitising a bound volume, it is important to support the lowest side of the book but, at the same time, ensure that any supports are not visible. Good materials to use are Plastazote, foam or black card. Make sure that you have a supply of these materials when you digitise.

The same principles are true when you photograph an insert from a book. It is important that it rests flat and that the materials do not interfere with the image. Look at the earlier examples and see how the good shots were achieved.

The following images show some other considerations when digitising a book:

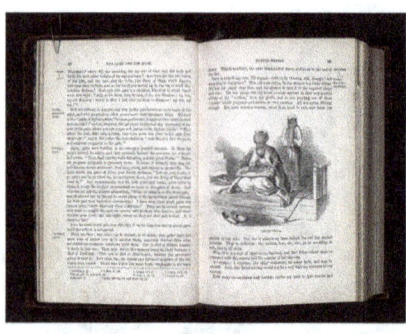

✓

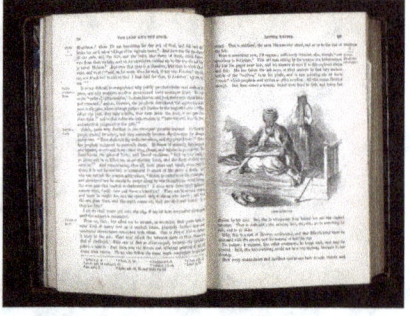

✗ If there is a shadow in the gutter of the book then turn the book 90 degrees so that the lights are opposite the shadow, thereby eliminating it. If the page needs to be held down, use the end of a piece of Perspex or any other clear hard plastic.

3. Image Standards 107

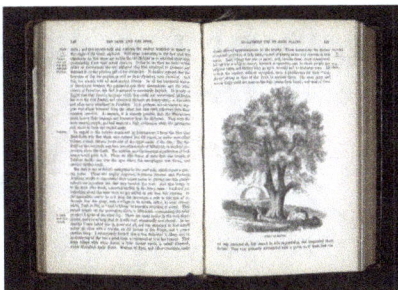

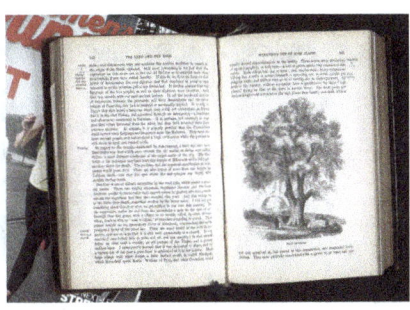

✓ If it is necessary, prop up one side of the book, then use a piece of the same black paper that you use for the background directly under the propped-up side of the book.

✗ Do not use other publications to prop up one side of the book.

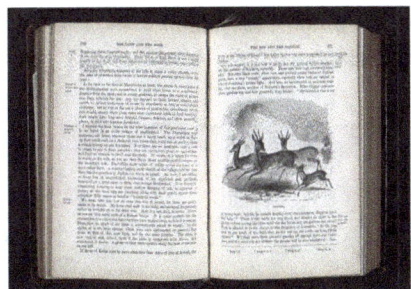

✓

✗ Do not use your fingers to flatten pages.

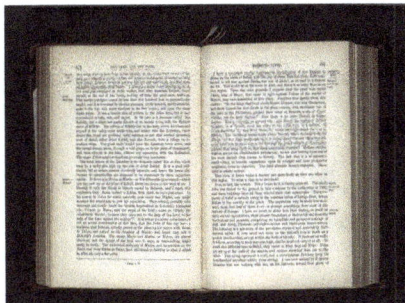

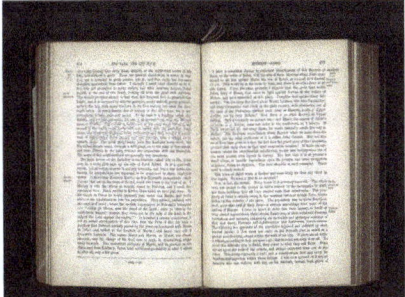

✓ If you need to use glass and find you have reflections, then use a piece of black paper and cut a hole to fit the lens through. Lowering the height of the lights will also reduce reflections.

✗ Ensure that there is no reflection from your light source. Refer to Figure 29 to see how this can be done.

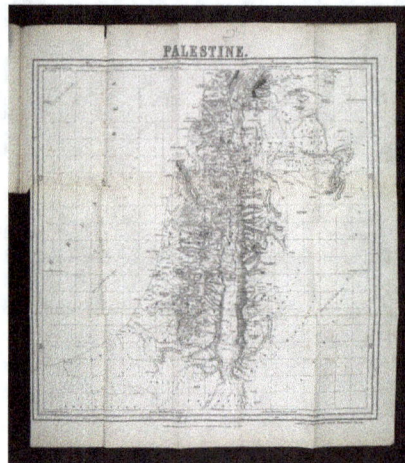 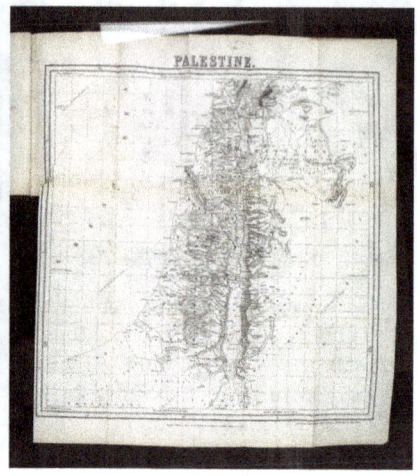

✓   ✗ If a publication contains a folded insert, ensure it rests flat.

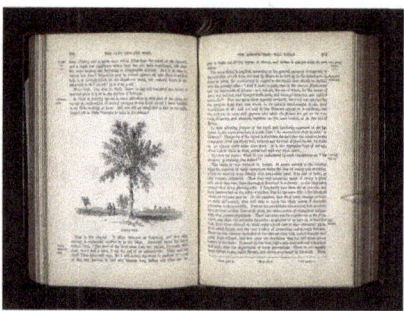 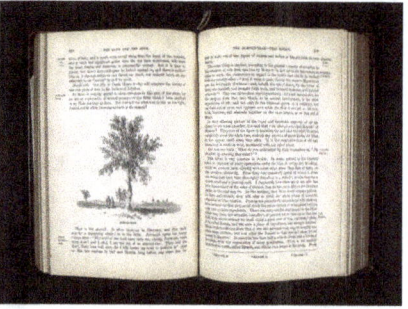

✓ Try putting small pieces of Plastazote under the edges of a book to make the double opening level, and if necessary hold down any parts that are lifting up with a Perspex strip. Don't use a wide-angle lens because this causes the image to look distorted.

✗ Make sure the pages are flat. Use a Perspex pointer if needed to gently press on the edge of the page.

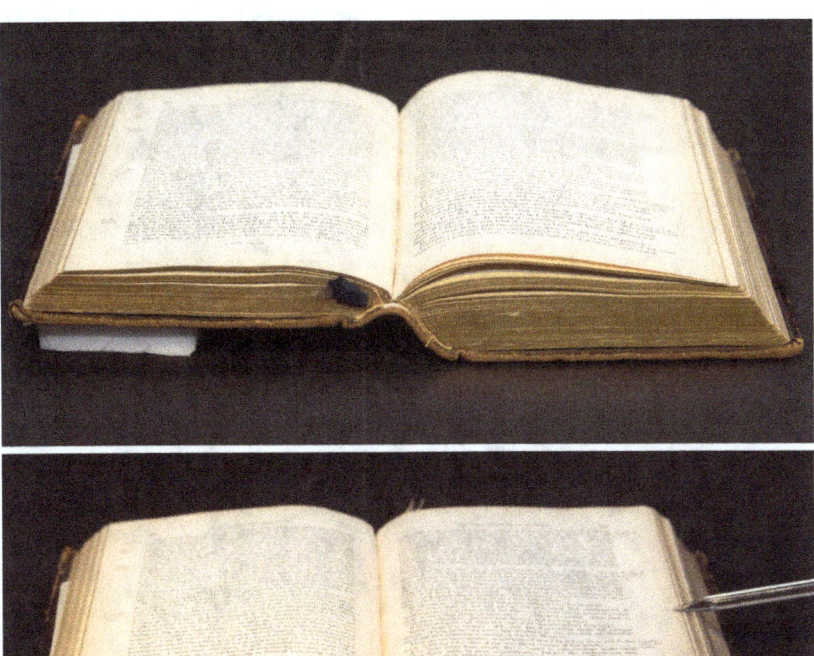

Figure 30. Building up foam beneath a bound book with a tight spine. This means it rests flat, with the object page parallel to the camera. The use of a Perspex pointer ensures that the page does not move during the taking of the photograph. Photos © Elizabeth Hunter, CC BY 4.0.

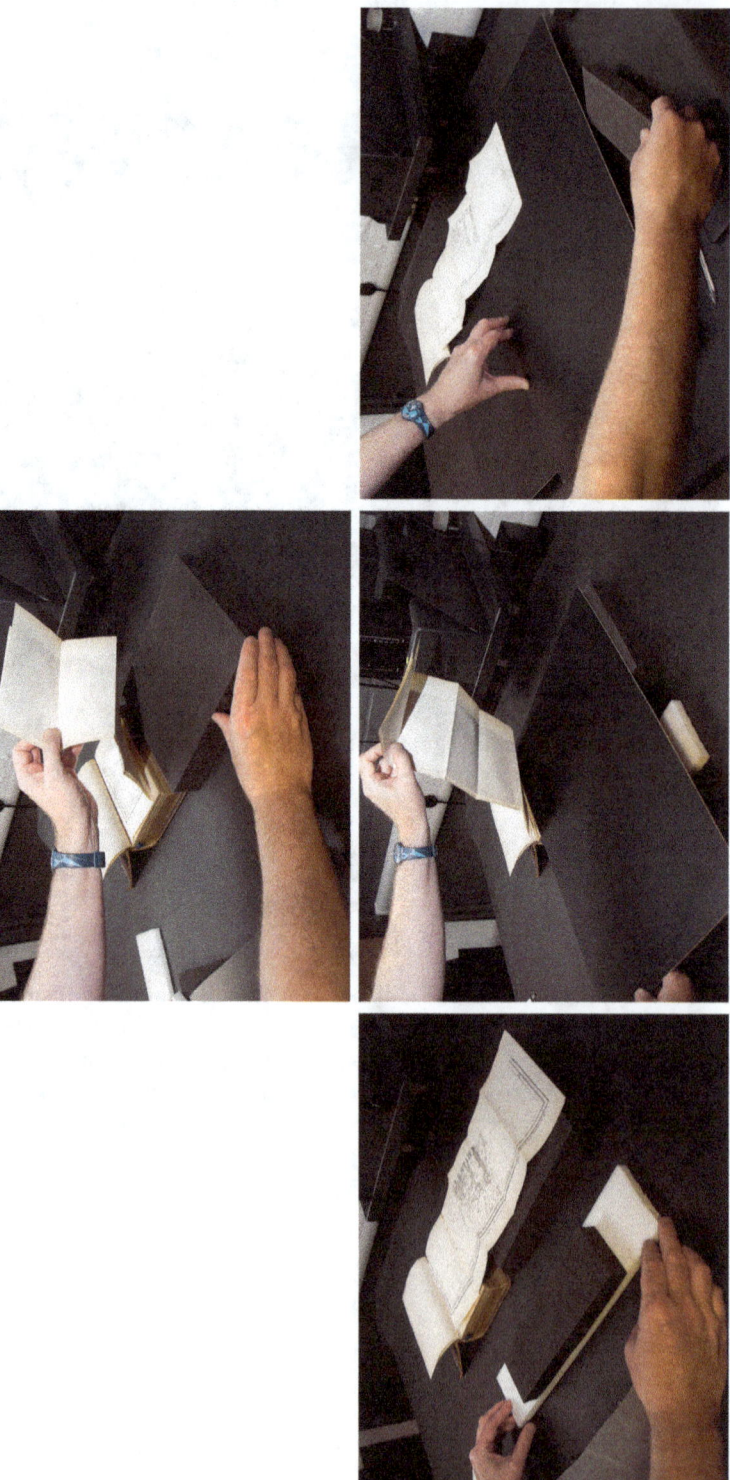

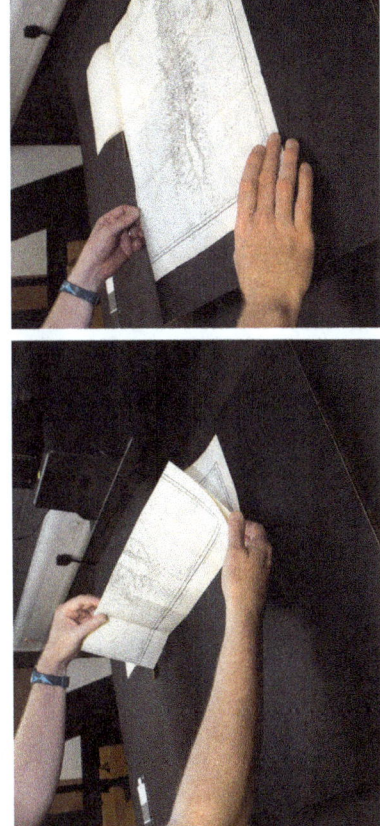
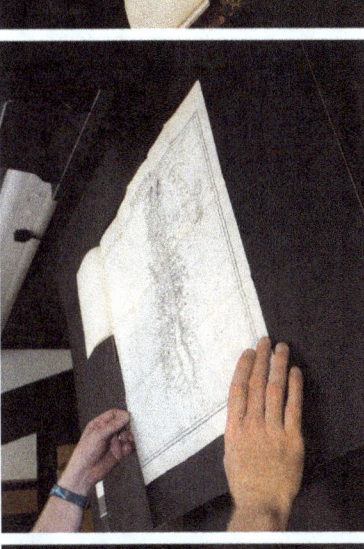
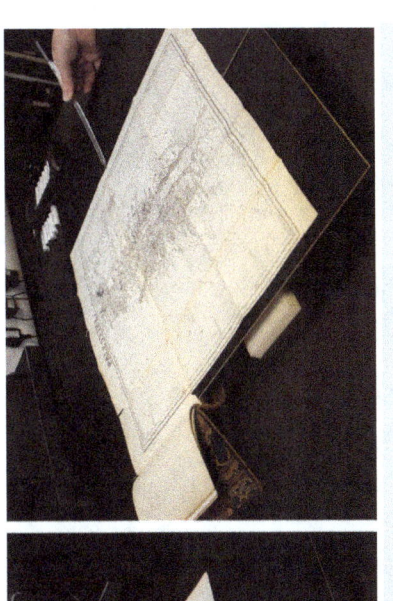

Figure 31. Step-by-step method for opening and supporting a folded map that is included within a bound book. This sequence shows the need for a careful and systematic approach. Photos © Elizabeth Hunter, CC BY 4.0.

4. Collection care and document handling

Flavio Marzo

Although the main focus of this book concerns the task of digitisation, the safety and care of the target collections is paramount. This chapter therefore provides a brief outline of conservation principles and methods.

General considerations for safe handling of library material

The primary aim of **safe handling** within digitisation projects is to minimise any further deterioration of the items being digitised.

- **All handling** has the potential to cause damage by exposing items to some level of wear and tear.
- **Don't rush.** Damage can be caused if items are roughly handled when trying to hurry.
- Always **lift** items rather than push or drag them across surfaces.
- Handle items as little as possible and assume all items are **fragile** and handle accordingly.
- Don't lift or **carry too much** by hand.
- Keep your working space tidy and free from food and drink.

> The document proprietors did not allow unbinding of volumes, so the originals were captured as if pages of a book. The originals were returned in the same condition as we had been given them. This kind of behaviour was important to affirm archival partner confidence.
>
> *Fernando Valle, EAP726, Peru*

Gloves or no gloves?

- Hands should be **clean, dry & free from grease**. Oils from balm can cause stains if transferred to items.
- Wearing gloves, especially cotton ones, **reduces manual dexterity** and the **sense of touch**, increasing the tendency to 'grab' items, thus increasing the risk of damage. Gloves **can pick up dirt** and transfer it to other items and to imaging devices, which often makes washing hands more effective.
- Gloves should be used when handling certain materials, like lead seals and metal objects, or when touching varnished surfaces, as in the case of globes. Gloves (nitrile gloves are advisable) are sometimes used when viewing photographs that, whenever possible, should be housed in protective sleeves or mounts to avoid direct contact with the fingers. Nitrile gloves are also recommended when handling negatives and glass plates.
- The British Library's Medieval manuscripts blog hosts a useful post that discusses this more fully and includes links to a video and further advice: http://blogs.bl.uk/digitisedmanuscripts/2011/08/white-gloves-or-not-white-gloves.html

Dirty and dusty material

Dust on items can compromise the quality of the digital surrogate. Extensive treatments should not be carried out by non-professional conservators, but light surface cleaning can be easily done by photographers or general project staff. Superficial dirt can be removed by brushing it with soft hair brushes. Always be careful to avoid abrasion of the surface being cleaned. When brushing the outside of bound volumes, the edges of the book-block need to be brushed from the spine towards the fore-edge of the book, avoiding piling dirt against the leather cover or even damaging the head or tail of the binding.

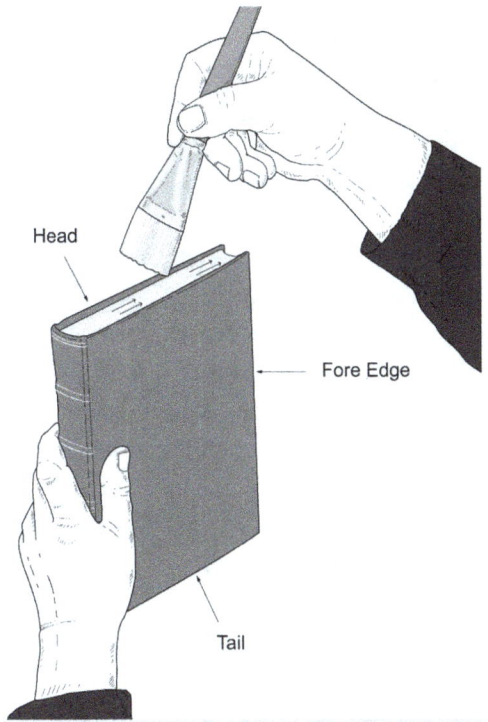

Figure 32. Diagram showing the correct brushing direction for a bound volume.
Illustration © Anne Leaver, CC BY 4.0.

Pictures and glass plate negatives

Handling. Always wear protective gloves, possibly made of nylon or latex, when handling glass plate negatives or pictures to avoid mechanical damage, such as breakages, fingerprints, and scratches. In addition to helping prevent contaminants (such as oils or acids from skin) being transferred to the plates, wearing gloves also protects hands from their potentially sharp edges.

Minimal cleaning. Keep cleaning to a minimum. Remove accumulated dust and surface dirt with a soft brush. Do not treat glass plate negatives with organic solvents, such as alcohol, or in aqueous solutions to clean them. To remove the majority of this dirt, the plates can be lightly dusted with a soft brush or a hand-held bulb duster (air blower) before digitisation. However, it is important to consider the condition of the glass plate before dusting, as dusting can damage the image if the emulsion is deteriorating or flaking.

Imaging. To help prevent possible particles of dust from scratching the plates or even the glass of the scanner, a transparent Mylar or acetate sheet can be placed over the scanner bed. This, together with taking care when placing plates onto the scanner, will protect both the scanner glass and the plates from being damaged.

Glass plate negatives (see page 78) can break due to the pressure exerted on them by the lid of the scanner during their digitisation. This can be avoided by raising the hood of the scanner slightly (approx. 1–5mm is ideal) if the lid opening can be adjusted, or by placing felt, foam, or cardboard strips around the edges of the scanner bed to cushion and lift the lid. This will also remove the risk of the plate being sucked up and dropped (due to the glass-on-glass suction effect) by the hood when the scanner is opened.

Loose-leaf items

Archival files can be made entirely of loose pages or can be fastened together. Fastenings like treasury tags, metal clips, pins or tapes can slow down the imaging process and endanger items during handling (e.g. by tearing the paper as pages are turned). It is thus advisable, sometimes, to remove them. The removal of fastenings may increase the risk of misplacement, dissociation and looting of pages but will make their handling safer.

Housing the files in new folders when fastenings are removed is a good way to mitigate those risks. A good quality four-flap folder, even if it does not entirely remove the threats mentioned, will mitigate them and guarantee much safer future storage for the now loose-leaf items.

Bound items

Bound items can be challenging to digitise due to their complex structural nature. Opening them can be difficult due to tight sewing or thick spine lining, and this can make the digitisation challenging or even impossible, since the integrity of the items should always be of paramount consideration.

To minimise the handling of bound items only one page should be photographed at a time. All the margins and the gutter of the page should be visible. Also, where possible, the sewing thread passages (middle of the section) should be visible, information that could be used as visual reference for the location of the shot within the quire (a bound section of the book) and the virtual reconstruction of a bound volume.

The sequence of shots, to minimise handling, should be done from the front to the back cover (all the rectos of the folios) and subsequently from back to front (all the versos), so that the volume is turned over only once.

A book support should always be used to hold a bound volume in place and to keep the opening at a suitable angle that enables image capture without straining or damaging the book structure.

Aims of the book support:

- To keep a bound volume opened comfortably to an angle never wider than 120 degrees.
- To restrain the opening, without causing damage (abrasion/tears) to the pages during imaging, while helping the photographer to turn them easily and efficiently.
- To move the entire volume, already secured onto the support, without having to drag it on the table surface.

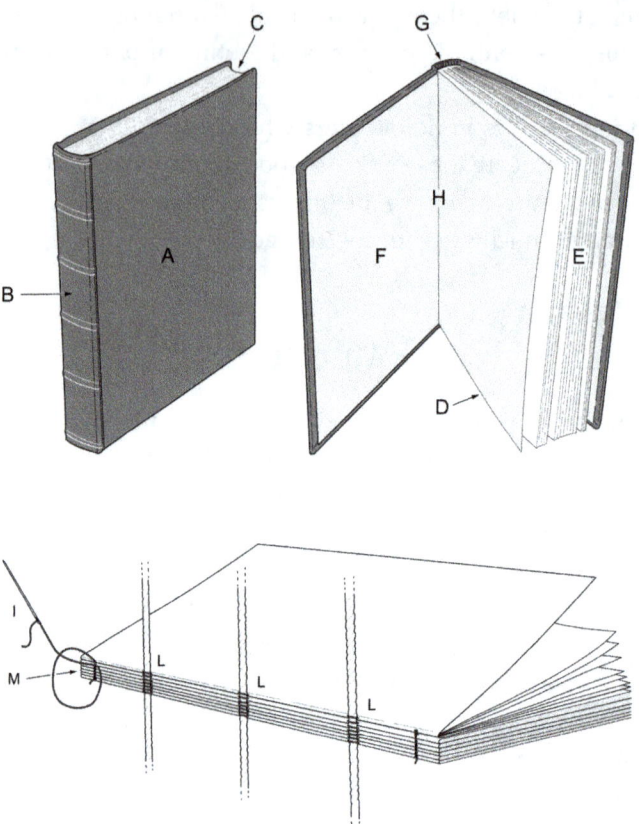

Figure 33. Book diagram and book binding terminology.
(A) Board (this drawing relates to western style bindings where the left board is at the front. In Islamic style bindings, where the text is from right to left, this is reversed); **(B)** Spine (the drawing depicts three raised bands and four panels); **(C)** Head-edge of the book-block; **(D)** Tail-edge of the book-block; **(E)** Fore-edge of the book-block; **(F)** Left inner board; **(G)** Head-band (*end-band* at head) with head-cap (*end-cap* at head); **(H)** Left inner joint; **(I)** Sewing thread with needle; **(L)** Sewing supports (single cords); **(M)** Sections. Illustrations © Anne Leaver, CC BY 4.0.

Housing

'Housing' refers to the mode of storage for any given document, whether a box, folder, or indeed anything else in which it is kept. It is essential to be able to achieve the best environment for the items, but without wasting time or resources — both of which can be very limited when working in the field or other remote circumstances. Customisable, archival-quality storage is a good solution to many issues and can improve the long-term preservation of items without the need for a great investment of time and money.

The archival quality of the materials a storage device is made of is the result of a production process that guarantees their long-term chemical and physical stability. Acid-free is a common label for this type of material, especially referring to paper and board, although it is by no means the only specification required for them to meet international standards such as ISO 16245:2009 or ISO 9706:1994. Other than paper and board, polyester film (Mylar, Melinex) and Tyvek are well-established preservation materials.

- ☐ Ready-made new folders can be acquired; folders need to be strong but easy to use and simple to assemble. Four flap folders made of light archival board with string and button(s) are very good; those folders need to have many ready-creased lines along the flaps so that they can be folded to the size of the object they have to contain, thus wrapping it tightly.

- ☐ When an item is not being used, it should be kept in its box or folder. The folder enclosures need to be tightly secured to avoid any movement inside, but at the same time, they should not be so tight that the excessive pressure causes the item to become distorted.

5. A workflow for digitisation

This chapter sets out a workflow for a digitisation project. It considers the entire process, from setting up, through digitisation, to file export, backing up and final deposit of a digital archive. This workflow should be considered as a guide rather than a prescriptive order, since every project will be slightly distinct from the next. The first elements of the workflow are perhaps those most liable to need adaptation. What is presented here refers to the digitisation of a collection that is held in one repository, and where the materials are digitised at a single central location. Arrangements would clearly have to be different in an itinerant project, where the photographer travels to the documents, and some of the check-in/check-back systems would probably be irrelevant.

The workflow can be divided into a five-stage process:

- preparation;
- creation of the digital images;
- renaming and organising the digital images;
- exporting the digital images;
- backing up.

To read more on the digitisation process see also Digital Appendix 3 at https://doi.org/10.11647/OBP.0138.11

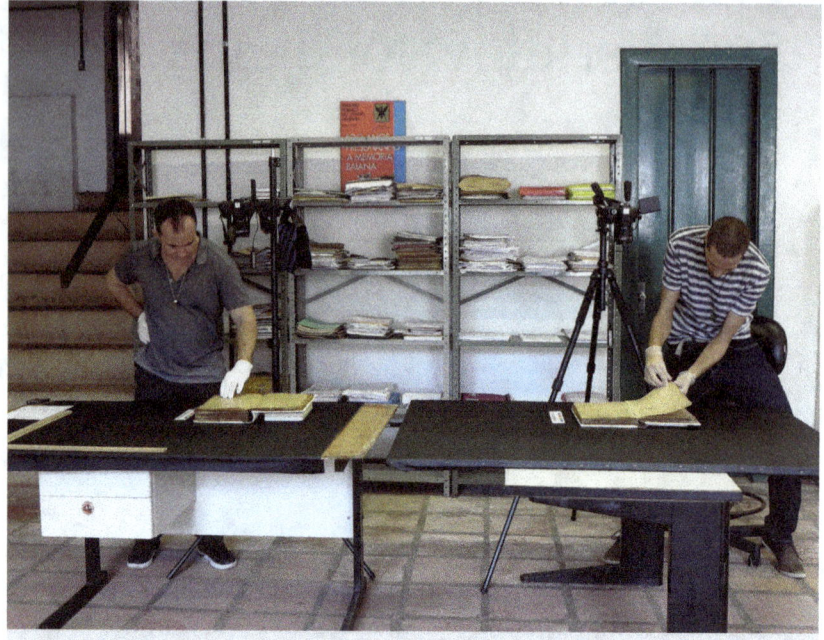

Figure 34. EAP703, Digitising notary books in Bahia, Brazil. Photo © João Reis, CC BY 4.0.

Preparation

This stage involves work with the original collection, in order to prepare it for digitisation. It also includes the setting up of the systems that will track the location of individual documents, and the progress of the project as a whole.

Ordering the collection

As far as circumstances permit, it is advisable for digitisation to address a collection whose composition is understood and which is reasonably well-ordered. At its most basic, this means that every document in the collection is known and can be digitised. Meanwhile, on a day-to-day basis, it makes the finding of individual documents a quick and easy task, as opposed to an inefficient, time-consuming exercise.

Where a project targets a catalogued collection that exists within a well-organised archive, this work will be unnecessary. However, in an unsorted collection, a list will be needed to at least the level of individual volume titles. Without this, it will be impossible to track overall progress, or even to know when the task of digitisation is finished.

While this list is essential, it is recognised that circumstances may not always allow the physical reorganisation of the collection. The place of storage may be too small, for example, or the custodian may not permit you to move items about. If so, this is a situation you will just have to cope with as best you can.

Control systems

Document tracking. If removing documents from a store, and particularly if they are being taken to a different venue to be digitised, it is necessary to have an audit trail for their location. This is essential because:

- ☐ it shows where every document is at any given time;
- ☐ it protects the original custodian, who is letting the document out of their control;
- ☐ it protects you, as you are taking possession of the document and thus have become responsible for its care.

This tracking can be achieved by a simple check-in/check-back form, an example of which is given in Figure 35. Here, for every individual document there is a pair of signatures required when it is removed from the archive, and a second pair when it is returned. Assuming that this form is always used, there can never be any doubt as to what document is where, or any ambiguity about who currently holds responsibility for it. Should a document go missing, the form will show the date of its movement and its last known location.

A parallel measure is to insert a labelled marker into the place in the shelf from which the item has been removed. This again will clearly show what items are not present. When the item is returned, the marker is removed.

If thought appropriate, the signees may also verify the condition of the document at the times of its issue and return. In the event of any damage occurring, this may indicate the point that it came about (and therefore under whose custody). Caution is needed, however, as original condition and subsequent 'damage' may be difficult to define or agree upon, particularly if one party does not see the document for a long time. The system must only be there to identify documents that are in an obviously poor condition at the time of issue, and to flag up any gross instances of damage to a document on its return.

Document name	Date removed from archive	Signed: Archivist	Signed: Project staff	Date returned to Archive	Signed: Archivist	Signed: Project staff
WILLS 1763-87	2/2/16	*sig*	A.P.	4/2/16	*sig*	A.P.
COMMON RECORDS	4/2/16	*sig*	A.P.	5/2/16	*sig*	A.P.
SUPREME COURT 1874	8/2/16	*sig*	A.P.	10/2/16	*sig*	A.P.
SHIPS BONDS 1849-49	10/2/16	*sig*		13/2/16	*sig*	
WILLS 1787-1805	13/02/16	*sig*	*sig*			

Figure 35. Example document tracking form.
Photo © Andrew Pearson, CC BY 4.0.

Document name	Digitized	Checked	Feedback	Corrections supplied	Exported (to TIFF)	Checksums created	Backed up	To British Library	Comments
Deed Book 1770	✓	✓	✓	n/a	✓	✓	✓	✓	
Deed Book 1771-72	✓	✓	✓	✓	✓	✓	✓		Pp. 25 and 26 out of focus: replacement images taken.
Deed Book 1776	✓	✓	✓	n/a	✓	✓			
Wills 1780-82	✓	✓	✓	awaited					p. 92 missing; new image requested
Deed Book 1777	✓								
Deed Book 1788-89	✓								

Figure 36. Example digitisation tracking form.
Illustration © Andrew Pearson, CC BY 4.0.

Project tracking. This element of tracking is purely for internal project use. It comprises a list containing every item to be digitised, with each line showing the state of progress for a particular document. The exact structure of the form will vary according to the project. In the example in Figure 36, the form deals with a situation in which the digital photographs are being taken by local staff, then checked by their line-manager (in this case the project director). Rather than being printed and hand-signed (as for the document tracking sheet), this document is best maintained on computer as it will be constantly in flux.

The exact structure of the form will vary according to the project. In this example, the form deals with a situation where the digital photographs are being taken by local staff, then checked by their line-manager (in this case the project director). Feedback is given on the digital images (identifying any issues of quality or composition, for example) and, where errors are found, replacement images are taken. The column for backing up refers to the project backup system, while the next column records whether the image set for that document has been migrated to the British Library's server. Only when all boxes are ticked (as for the 1770 Deed Book) can the work on the document be considered complete.

Transport

This issue will only be relevant if digitisation is being carried out somewhere other than the documents' place of storage. Where this is the case, the logistics are worth considering in advance — for example:

- How far will the documents need to be moved? Can you carry them by hand or will you need a vehicle?
- What will you carry the document(s) in? Are they already in suitable containers (e.g. an archive box in good condition) or will you have to buy/bring something for this task?
- How many documents will you move at once (and therefore have away from their usual place of storage)?
- What other factors might limit or affect the transport process? For example, is the archive store only open at certain hours or on particular days? Is your work location prone to heavy rain or other bad weather, such that it could be unacceptable to move documents at given times (and possibly for long periods)?

Creation of the digital images

Setting up

- ☐ Create the computer folder for the digital images for this particular document.
- ☐ Turn the camera and lights on.
- ☐ If using tethered shooting, activate the software and the Live View window.
- ☐ Set the camera settings (image format, aperture, shutter speed, ISO — as required).
- ☐ If using tethered shooting, specify the destination folder for the images.
- ☐ Lay out the document ready for photographing, and place the colour-checker cards.

Photographing

- ☐ Photograph an ID Shot.

This is a form on which you record the details of the document to be digitised. It provides the key means of identifying the digital images that are about to be taken: even if the files are subsequently mis-named, this form will allow you to see which document they relate to. As a minimum, the form should state the project name and/or code, and the document name, title or code. Other information can be useful, such as the date of digitisation and the name of the photographer, plus any other comments you may wish to record (for example, about the document's condition, or the circumstances of the photography).

- ☐ Begin photographing the document, starting with the spine and front cover for bound volumes.[1]

---

[1] An alternative photography method, which involves the shooting of all odd pages first, followed by the even pages in reverse order, is outlined in Digital Appendix 1. While more complex and potentially prone to error, this method has the advantage of reducing the amount of handling needed during the photography process.

- After 10 photographs, use an image browser to check: are the images in the correct format? Is the document layout satisfactory? Is the image quality and focus good? Assuming yes, you may proceed to the remainder of the document. If anything is not satisfactory, delete the images, make the necessary corrections, and reshoot from the beginning.
- Continue photographing to the end of the document, finishing with the back cover for bound volumes.
- Photograph a Condition/Comment Sheet.

This latter form has several functions. First, it will clearly show that digitisation of this volume is complete (this is obvious for bound volumes, but far less so for unbound documents). Second, it is a useful place to record detail needed for cataloguing, particularly about the document's physical characteristics, e.g. the number of pages or folios and the volume's dimensions. Finally, since every page has now passed under your eyes, you may record any other observations made during photography, for example the document's general condition, or the presence or extent of water or insect damage.

Checking and correcting

- Open the photographs in an image browser.
- Browse through the files in order and confirm that no pages have been missed (this is easily done by checking that the gutter of a bound volume alternates with each image).
- Identify any images where the quality, layout or sharpness of focus is not adequate.
- Re-photograph any missing pages, and pages with errors.

If a replacement image is shot, the original file needs to be removed and the new image stitched into the identical place in the sequence. (For example, if the photograph of page 72 is incorrect, you must delete it, then rename the replacement such that it will appear in the file sequence between the images for pages 71 and 73.)

Renaming and organising the digital images

During this stage, the file names are changed from those generated by the camera (e.g. DSC 001) to names that are specific to the document you have photographed. Renaming files manually is impractical and simple software packages exist that can do this operation for large batches of files.

- ☐ Import the files into the batch renaming software.

At this stage you must confirm that the file sequence is correctly sorted — i.e. that it begins with the ID shot, and proceeds page by page through to the back cover and End/Condition form. Sorting options include by name, date/time taken, or by attributes (e.g. file type, size). **It is crucial that your sequence is sorted by file name**, as the alternatives could order your files in a different sequence — i.e. one that bears no relation to the order of the original document.

- ☐ Specify the new name to be applied to the sequence.

Usually this will comprise the project code and document title, followed by the photograph number. By doing this, you create a unique identifier for each of the files, one that will not be duplicated within your project or by any other. Thus, for example, for the project EAP 794, the photographs for Deed Book 1834 are named as EAP794_Deed_Book_1834_001, followed by 002, 003, and so on.

Developing vs editing

Developing and editing are two distinct processes. Digital developing comprises the adjustment of the image, for example of colour or contrast, in much the same way as film would be processed in a dark room. Changes are made, but the actual content of the image remains unaltered. This is distinct from editing, where the content itself is altered: for example, by airbrushing. Given that the purpose of archive digitisation is to faithfully record the artefact and its information, **making any such alterations or elisions is entirely unacceptable.**

Developing and exporting the digital images

During this stage the RAW files are exported to a suitable output format (always TIFF for EAP projects). This creates a parallel set of files: the original RAW files are not overwritten.

Importing

- ☐ Import the files into the photo processing software (e.g. Lightroom).
- ☐ Confirm that the sequence is sorted by name (as above, not by date/time taken or any other attribute).

Developing (optional sub-step)

- ☐ If necessary, rotate the images to the correct orientation. (N.B. EAP expects all images to be supplied to it in the correct orientation.)
- ☐ Carry out any developing processes.

Image software allows for numerous adjustments to be made, comparable to the development processes of a darkroom for film photography. Generally, only the most basic developing would be undertaken for an EAP project: for example, to correct the colour balance (by means of sampling the colour checker card) or applying lens calibration (which can be used to square up images that are warped by wider-angle photography — though only to an extent). As far as possible, however, avoid this step or do an absolute minimum: 'developing' your images may make them more pleasing (to your eye, at least), but risks taking them further from the original — which is, after all, what you are attempting to record. Bear in mind also that the receiving or funding organisation may not accept images that have had extensive or inappropriate development applied to them.[2]

Exporting

- ☐ Create the destination folder for the images to be exported to.
- ☐ Export the images to the required format.

---

2   This includes EAP.

☐ Once the export process is complete (this may take several hours, depending on the number of files) check the product: is the file type correct, with the specified attributes? Are the correct number of files present? Is the file order correct?

Creating checksums

Checksums are used to ensure the integrity of a file after it has been transmitted from one storage device to another: for example, between your primary dataset and any subsequent external backup. A checksum is created by a checksum calculator program and is appended to the dataset to which it relates (a checksum may be created for a single file, or for groups of files: for example, a complete folder of photographs). At any later point, the checksum programme may be used to verify the integrity of the data (whether the original dataset or a copy or backup). The program compares the checksum against the data: even a tiny change to the dataset will result in a completely different checksum value, generating an error report. Larger changes will also be identified: for example, a missing file.[3] **EAP requires a checksum for every digital folder of images**.

Backing up

Data loss is an inescapable reality of the digital age. Everybody reading this book will have lost electronic files at some point, whether the latest version of a document, a few personal photographs, or something of larger proportions.

The purpose of archive digitisation is to safeguard the information contained within documents that are at risk of destruction, either through natural or human agency. The survival of some collections may be uncertain even in the immediate future; others may be so poorly preserved that handling for photography may be possible once, and

---

3   As a word of caution, certain computer applications can occasionally add 'hidden' files to a folder: for example, Windows Explorer may add a thumbs.db after files are viewed. If present, such files will cause the checksum program to identify a discrepancy, even though all of the image files are present and uncorrupted.

once only. It is therefore an imperative that the digital data generated from any physical collection is protected from loss.

Commercial companies and academic institutions have complex systems of data storage, both in-house and off-site, managed and maintained by specialist staff. Ultimately the digital data from your project will be migrated to such systems and, major catastrophes aside, will be permanently safeguarded. This section addresses the preceding period, while the data is being generated by, and in the sole possession of, your project. This is the stage at which the data is most vulnerable.

Principles

Backing-up is a crucial process that everyone should do in order to have a fail-safe. The principle is to make copies of particular data in order to use those copies for restoring the information if a failure occurs, whether due to deletion, corruption, theft or viruses. Some basic principles are as follows:

- **Back it up** as soon as possible. Never rely on a single copy for longer than you have to, whether it is on a camera memory card, a computer, CD or an external hard drive.
- **Split it up**. Even if you have made multiple copies, the dataset is still at significant risk while they are kept in the same location. Think about heading off the obvious worst-case scenarios. If your bag was mislaid or stolen while travelling, would all your data be lost with it? Could a fire at your property destroy all your copies? While in the field, consider how you might get around this risk, particularly in terms of loss in transit. As a minimum, split the copies across your bags (including hand and cabin baggage), and ideally across multiple people. Some other options include:
    - Leaving a copy with somebody local, to be retrieved later, or posted on if your copies are lost or destroyed.
    - Uploading the data to Dropbox or a data-sharing website.
    - Posting a second copy of the data to yourself.
- **Keep control** of your backups. Have a primary dataset from which all backups are generated. It is no good making multiple copies,

but doing so in such a chaotic way that you have no idea which is the current and most up-to-date version.

- **Use backup software.** Simple and inexpensive programs exist that will copy data. Never use the manual 'copy/paste' or 'drag/drop' methods: these are too prone to user error.

Types of backup

There are three principal forms of replicating data: backup, mirror, and synchronisation. In the following discussion, the original dataset is termed the Source; the place to which it is copied is termed the Destination.[4]

Initially, replication will begin with a simple copying process, as the files from the Source are duplicated in a new empty Destination. After this point the different types of replication will lead to different outcomes.

Synchronisation

In Synchronisation, files are copied in both directions (from Source to Destination, and vice-versa), creating identical datasets with everything held in both. This is commonly used by home-users, particularly for their music collections. However, it is not recommended for backing up the data from a digitisation project, since it is advisable to have a one-way process, from your Source dataset (which you may be modifying and updating) to the Destination.

Backup

A Backup copies files in one direction: from the Source to the Destination. It does not involve the deletion of files. Because of this, after the initial copying, the Destination will not be a duplicate of the original dataset. Rather, it will be larger, containing files that have been deleted or renamed on the Source. Backups have the advantage that

---

4 The definitions given here are derived from the website for the backup software program Syncback.

data accidentally deleted from the Source can be retrieved from the Destination. On the other hand, backup datasets become increasingly large as time progresses, including numerous files that are superfluous or out-of-date, and which have been deliberately removed from the Source.

Mirror

Mirror is a backup that also replicates deletions (to be more accurate, 'absences') on the Source to the Destination (i.e. it removes 'orphans'). Mirroring therefore ensures that the Destination contains exactly the same files as the Source, and nothing else. It is not the same as a simple Backup because it deletes files. It is also not the same as synchronisation because it only copies files in one direction.

Using a Mirror profile requires you to accept the risk that accidental deletions from the Source will also be removed on the Destination. If you delete a file by mistake, and don't realise until after the next backup run, then that file will be irretrievably lost. Its advantage is that it creates a minimal-size dataset which will comprise only the current project files.

Table 4. Summary of backup rules.
Based on profile descriptions from Syncback SE.

Backup	Mirror
Files will be copied from Source to Destination	Files will be mirrored from Source to Destination
If the same file has been changed on both Source and Destination then the file on Source will replace the file on Destination	If the same file has been changed on both Source and Destination then the file on Source will replace the file on Destination
Files only on Source are copied to Destination	Files only on Source are copied to Destination
If a file is only on Destination then it is ignored	Files only on Destination are deleted

Backup or mirror?

Users must decide whether Backup or Mirror is the most appropriate method. As discussed above, both have advantages and disadvantages. However, the two may be used in parallel.

A basic, 'manual' method is to have two Destinations, one being a Backup, and the other a Mirror. Doing this makes for a somewhat more complicated data-management process, but it exploits the best attributes of both backup and mirror. On the backup destination you will have a complete dataset of every file you have ever created, enabling accidental deletions to be retrieved; on the mirror you will have a dataset which can be used to restore your current data, and which is a 'tidy' copy of the dataset which can be transferred to the receiving institution (which will not want extraneous files).

The same process can be done automatically with certain backup software programs. Backup protocols can be set up, such that when a file is changed/deleted on Source it will also be changed/deleted on the Destination *but will also* be put aside in a separate directory. This directory serves as insurance against accidental changes and deletions, though of course it will add (possibly very considerably) to the volume of backed-up data.

Never entrust a hard drive containing the day's data to anyone (including other team members) before you've copied the content to a secure place. Then, make an additional backup.

Michael Gervers, EAP 254, EAP340, EAP526, EAP704, Ethiopia

A 'digitising disaster' is never quite as bad as it seems at the time and it is always possible to come up with a solution!

Sophie Sarin, EAP488, EAP690 and EAP879, Mali

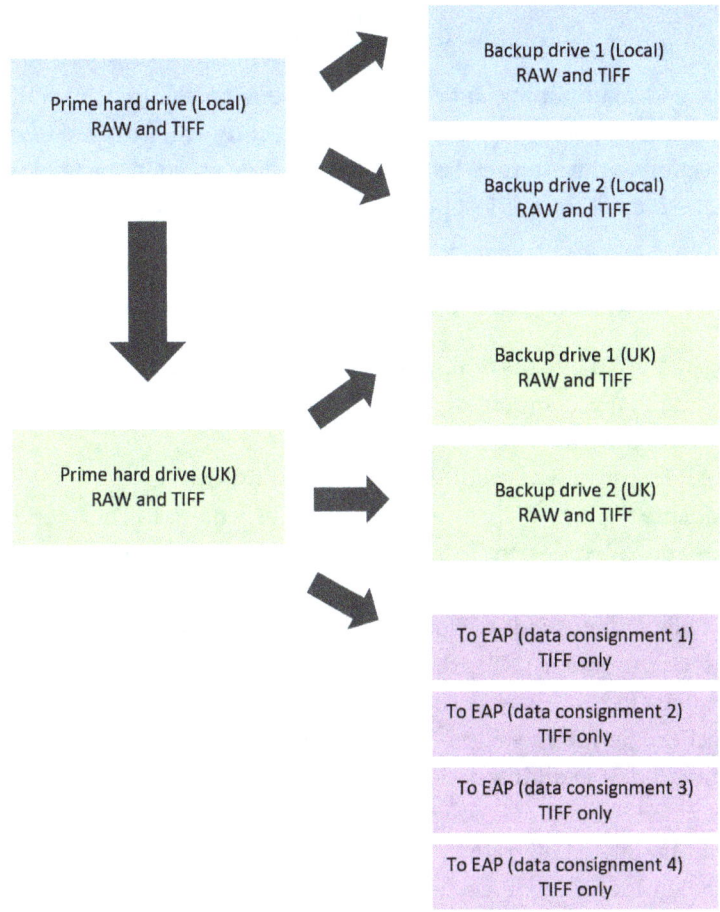

Figure 37. A field-based system for backup.
In this model, all work is being undertaken locally — i.e. photography, checking and data export to TIFF all occur at the place where the documents are held. The flow of data is therefore one-way only.
If only photography takes place locally, with checking and export to TIFF being undertaken remotely by the project manager (in this case in the UK), then the data flow will become more complex. RAW files will be transmitted to the UK, with the final TIFF datasets sent both back to the local drives, and onwards to the British Library.
In both scenarios, however, the principle remains the same: of safeguarding the data by holding multiple backups in separate locations. The final datasets are dispatched incrementally to EAP, as soon as a meaningful volume of images has been compiled. This means that the data is held only on the project hard drives for as little time as possible. Illustration © Andrew Pearson, CC BY 4.0.

Virus checking

Using and maintaining anti-virus software is an essential part of data protection. Wherever possible, keep the software up to date via a connection to the internet. If that is not possible when in the field, virus-scan the data at the earliest possible opportunity on your return.

Cataloguing/creation of metadata

Although not the focus of this book, cataloguing and the creation of the metadata that accompanies your digital images ('Listing') is an integral part of the process.

EAP has stringent requirements for Listing, and issues a pro-forma spreadsheet into which all details must be entered. The mandatory information includes: the location and ownership of the original records, including any issues relating to copyright; the institutions where the data will be deposited; the technical specification of the images created and the equipment used to create and manage them (i.e. the camera and computer software); cataloguing details at the level of Project, Collection, Series and File — the latter being each individual volume/document that is digitised. Some of the technical data is required at the point when the data is accessioned by EAP, while much of the catalogue will ultimately be migrated to the British Library's main catalogue.

The guidelines for correctly completing the Listing spreadsheet enter into considerable detail and fall outside the scope of this book. Nevertheless, several points do need to be emphasised:

- Do not underestimate how much time will be required for Listing — and certainly do not treat it as an afterthought!
- Study the Listing guidelines in advance, and in detail, so that you fully understand the requirements. If necessary, obtain copies of other projects' Listings, to serve as guidance (though remember that your spreadsheet must be the most recent version, so you cannot adopt an earlier version as an exact template).
- Listing cannot be done retrospectively (e.g. after the rest of the project is complete). Some elements can be worked through from the comfort of your office back at home, but many important

details — particularly about the physical characteristics of the materials — are practically impossible to determine remotely.

- In terms of workflow, the logical point at which to create the detailed cataloguing information is at the time of photography or — more precisely — immediately after you have finished digitising. The document is in your hands and is there to be measured and described. Each page has just passed under your eyes, so you will have been able to note any issues such as torn, stained or insect-damaged pages, or where pages are partially or completely missing.
- Back up the Listing spreadsheet as rigorously as you do your digital images. Re-entering the data for a large project could be incredibly time-consuming, and some information about the original documents may be difficult or impossible to retrieve from memory alone.

When all the necessary recording and data entry is done, you will have finished working with that particular document. Unless it is then to be the subject of conservation work, it can be returned to its archive or owner, and the process of digitising can move on to the next item.

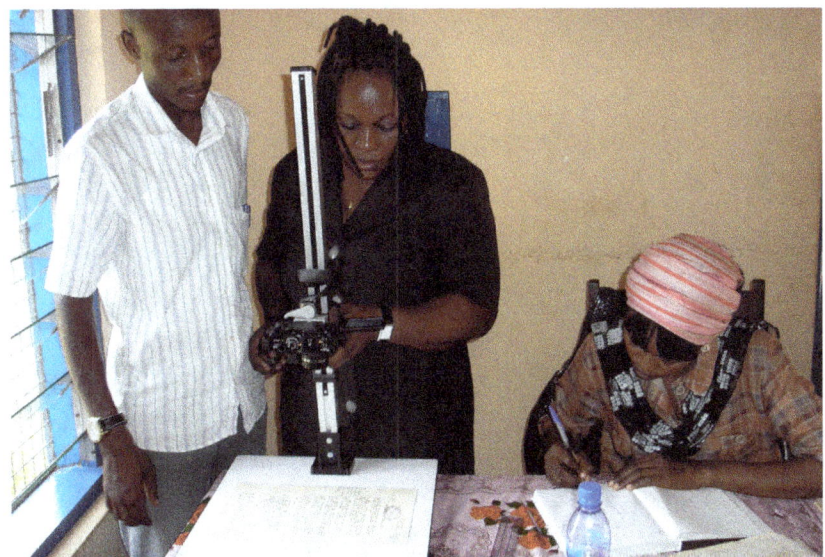

Figure 38. EAP256, Listing taking place alongside photography in Tamale, Ghana. Photo © Ismail Montana, CC BY 4.0.

6. On the ground

Where the preceding chapters have dealt with technical standards and processes, this chapter is concerned with on-the-ground practicalities. An alternative title might simply be 'getting it done'. What is offered here cannot ever be comprehensive, as each project will operate within a unique set of circumstances. Indeed, the best advice is to understand as much as possible about your own project before launch, and if you are travelling to deliver your project then be prepared to improvise when you get there! Nevertheless, knowledge is power, and in compiling this chapter we have drawn on the experience of numerous EAP grant holders, and hope to pull out some of the common themes. If nothing else, we hope it provides some food for thought.

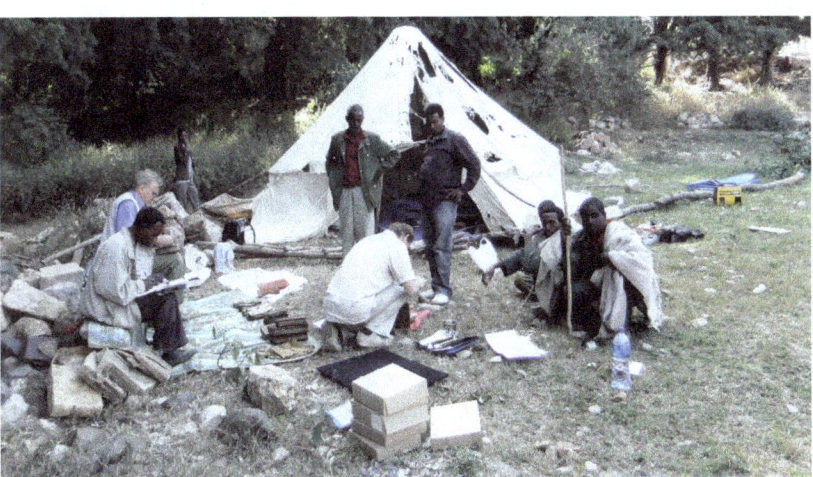

Figure 39. EAP526, Theory meets practical realities in Ethiopia. Photo © Michael Gervers, CC BY 4.0.

© Butterworth, Pearson, Sutherland and Farquhar, CC BY 4.0   https://doi.org/10.11647/OBP.0138.06

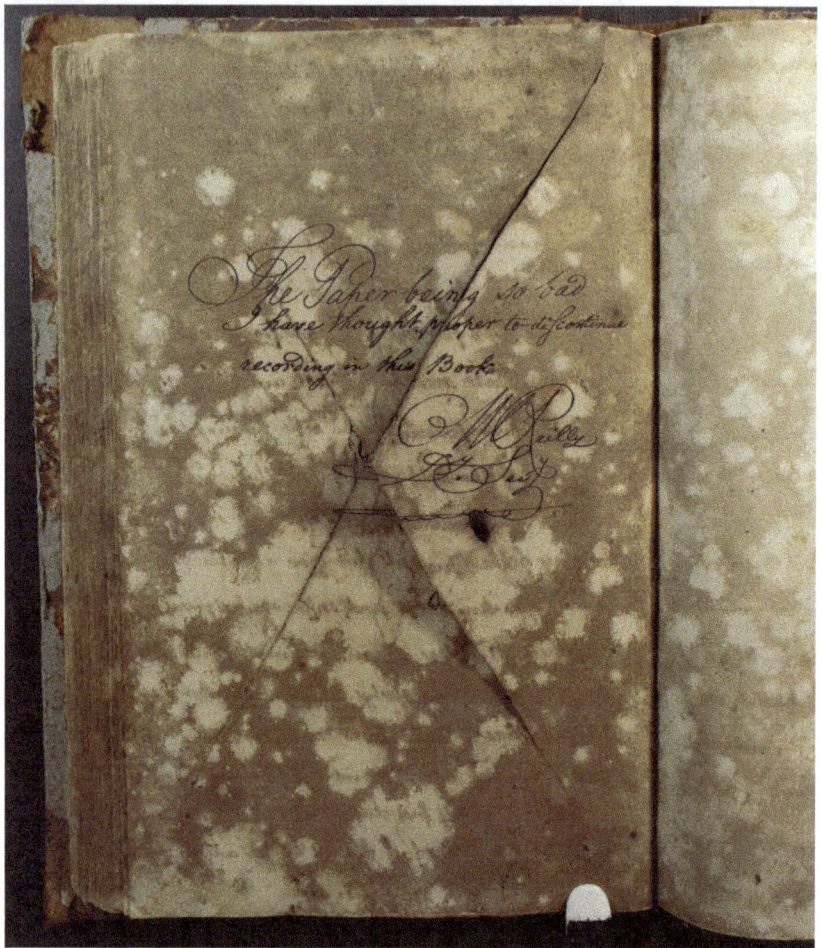

Figure 40. EAP688, Fragile subjects.
It is not only the local circumstances that will complicate your project; often the physical state of the materials themselves will pose significant challenges, as here in St Vincent. Photo © Kenneth Morgan, CC BY 4.0.

On nearly every expedition, one or more of the team members (including local participants) has been seriously ill, but usually for no more than three days. It is best to have the recommended inoculations before departure, and to take a supply of medications.

Michael Gervers, EAP 254, EAP340, EAP526, EAP704, Ethiopia

Before departure

The project team

Before departing for the project, you and your staff may require:

- visas;
- work permits;
- travel insurance (it is crucial that this includes cover for work-related activities);
- professional insurance (if required);
- immunisations.

Also consider the actual travel arrangements. Everything should be booked (flights, accommodation, airport transfers etc.). Any local partners should also be informed of the date and time of your arrival!

Health and safety

This is paramount. We all tolerate 'risk' in our everyday lives, but when undertaking a work-based project you have an additional responsibility to protect yourself and your staff. Failure to do so is simply unacceptable: it potentially exposes project personnel to danger, and yourself and your employer to prosecution for negligence.

If you are working for an academic institution or commercial company, these will have rules that require a formal risk assessment to be carried out. If not, undertake one anyway. This is not a box-ticking exercise, another burden of a bureaucratic age. Rather, it is an absolutely essential means of ensuring that you give due consideration to the theoretical dangers that you or your team may be exposed to. Risk assessments usually comprise four basic stages:

- an identification and quantification of risk (i.e. what potential dangers can you foresee, what is the worst-case outcome, and how likely are these to actually happen);
- formulation of control measures or 'mitigation' (i.e. the means by which you will avoid the dangers, reduce the likelihood of their occurrence, or lessen their potential impact);

> Working in semi-urban and rural areas of West Bengal itself is a painstaking task, purely due to bad roads and poor public transport networks. Added to that was the question of safety, while frequent power-cuts and road disruptions for political agitation or some other issue were part of daily life for our researchers.
>
> *Abhijit Bhattacharya, EAP643, Bengal*

> Check your insurance. If your employer is insuring you, make sure they are aware of what you are doing. Check if you have to submit a risk assessment. Alternatively, make sure that your personal insurance provides complete cover.
>
> *Tim Procter, EAP626, Sierra Leone*

> We have always found that to be successful when working in churches locally it is essential to travel with an ecclesiastic who is well known to, and respected by the community where one would like to work. In one case the bishop appointed the paymaster to accompany us. He was highly respected by the monks and remained with us nearly for the entire duration of the time we spent at the site. We were surprised one day to find that he carried a pistol in a shoulder holster under his smock.
>
> *Michael Gervers, EAP 254, EAP340, EAP526, EAP704, Ethiopia*

> Violence during electoral campaigns can seriously affect the viability of planned projects. Even with the help of the partner institution on the ground, tensions of this kind make it difficult to carry out an Endangered Archives project, especially if the documents are kept by public administration offices. Election dates can be changed unexpectedly.

> In my case, I had to postpone the activity on two occasions. I was delighted about the British Library's realistic approach; there are no pressures to proceed with planned schedules; the project is not lost. This is very positive.

- an assessment of 'residual risk' (i.e. those that remain after you have implemented control measures);
- an overall assessment of the acceptability of the project (i.e. while dangers will always remain, and accidents can always occur, are the risks now within acceptable parameters, both in terms of likelihood and severity of outcome?)

For those without experience of undertaking risk assessments, this process may seem abstract. However, it is little more than common sense: identifying a problem and finding a solution. Below are three examples:

- Lone working and travelling.
  Risk: if travelling somewhere remote, perhaps on poor roads, what would happen if you crashed your vehicle? How long would it be until you were missed?
  Control measures: adopt a Travel Safe Plan of Action (TSPA). This will set out the route you will follow and the time you expect to arrive. It should be lodged with somebody with whom you can confirm your safe arrival, or who can raise the alarm if you become badly overdue. Ensure your vehicle is roadworthy. Carry a mobile or satellite phone. Consider hiring a local driver who is experienced on these roads.
- Poor/unhealthy water supplies.
  Risk: contracting a waterborne disease.
  Control measures: buy bottled water; carry a water purification kit; carry anti-microbial drugs (making sure they are suitable for the disease environment you are working in: not every antibiotic is effective in every situation).
- Political instability/civil disturbance.
  Risk: danger of violence to project team.
  Here, no control measures are likely to be practical, since the situation is not within your control. Seek advice from your own government about whether it is advisable to travel. Seek advice from local people about the nature of the problem, how and where it is manifesting itself, and what could be done to stay out of trouble. A judgement can then be made about whether to proceed.

Your equipment

- Assemble all the kit and **test** it!

- Make sure you are totally **familiar** with how everything works, both in terms of hardware and software. Practice assembly, disassembly and cleaning.

- Undertake a **trial digitisation**. Try to make this trial sufficiently long and as 'real' as possible, to uncover any problems that could occur. The less learning and troubleshooting you have to do on site, the better.

- Consider **insuring** the equipment. This may or may not be feasible, as many insurers' requirements (for example about security) are too stringent for a remote or unusual project to be able to comply. Give yourself time to shop around, and if your project is in an unusual location expect your application to be referred to a broker. Read the insurer's small print and, when making the application, be totally transparent about what you will be doing. If your circumstances change at any stage (for example, moving your 'studio' from a specified place of work to a new location), it is essential that you inform the insurer to confirm the policy still applies.

- Related to the above, find out as much as you can about where you will be working. How secure (or otherwise) is it? What locks does it have? Are there window bars?

- In parallel, think about equipment **redundancy**. In other words, how will you deal with loss, damage, theft or confiscation? Do you have a backup plan, either by carrying a spare of every essential item, or are you confident that there are places locally where you could buy a compatible replacement?

> Much of our equipment was stolen from one of the archives on two separate occasions. Fortunately, we never kept all of the equipment in the same place at the same time. The first burglary left us with half the equipment and we only had one archive left, so that was fine. The final burglary left us with one set of equipment, but we were almost done.
>
> *Courtney Campbell, EAP627 and EAP853, Brazil*

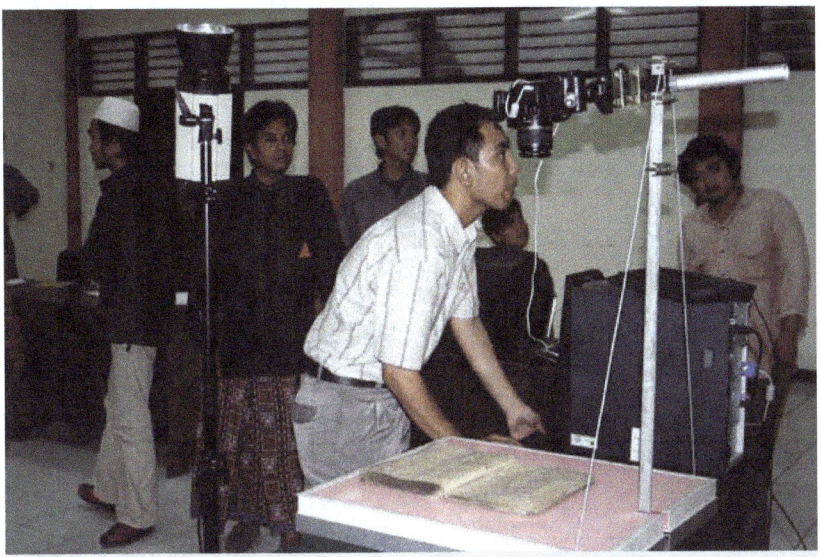

Figure 41. EAP061, A custom-made copy stand, Indonesia.
An ingenious solution to the lack of a copy stand. During this early EAP project, as in many since, grant holders have had to depart from the 'textbook' in order to get things done. Photo © Amiq Ahyad, CC BY 4.0.

Logistics

Working in distant, and possibly remote, locations requires thought to be given to logistics. In terms of equipment, this should be considered at an early stage because it may dictate what purchases you make, and where you make them.

- **Place of purchase.** As discussed above, it is advisable to buy, assemble and test the core digitising equipment prior to it being taken to its point of use. However, some items may be heavy or bulky, while it may not be permissible to transport others — for example, anything containing chemicals or solvents.[1] If such items are available for purchase locally, consider whether they are best bought on arrival.

---

1   Check, for example, whether a freight shipment can contain spare batteries. Often, batteries for cameras and computers are allowed to be transported within those pieces of equipment, but extra batteries (i.e. loose within the shipment) are prohibited.

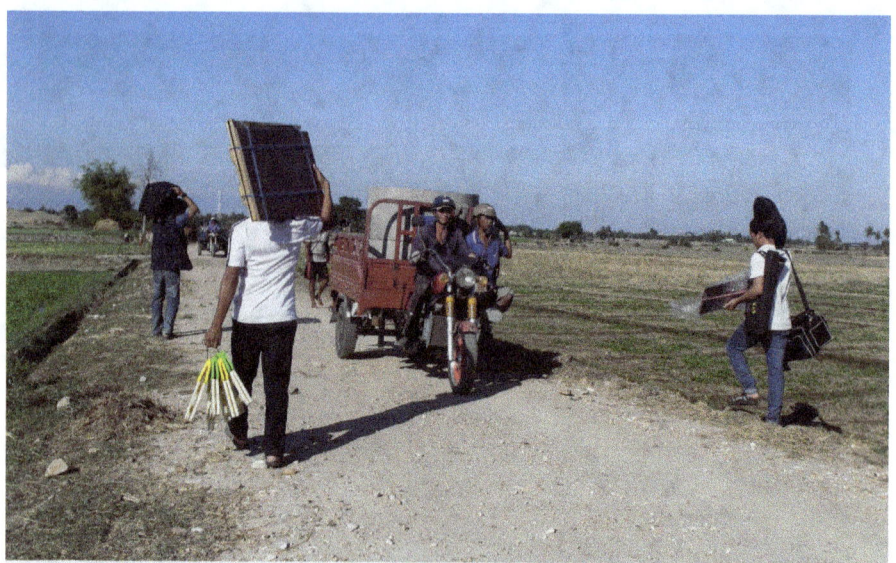

Figure 42. EAP698, On the road in Vietnam. Photo © Hao Phan, CC BY 4.0.

If you are shipping equipment by sea, try to find an experienced shipping agent with strong in-country connections, and make sure you know what the procedures are supposed to be at the receiving end.

Tim Procter, EAP626, Sierra Leone

Do not take the delivery times advertised by freight couriers on trust. For more unusual destinations, where a particular courier doesn't have its own supply network, 'guaranteed six-day delivery' may be closer to six weeks. This was my experience — despite using a very well-known company. Ask somebody at the destination which courier has a local office and a reputation for reliability.

I am regularly searched when entering the country and have to justify each piece of equipment. I have always been able to negotiate and have not, to date, had anything confiscated. This was particularly trying when I brought a laptop to donate to a state organisation: I was accused of subverting the rules even with the representative of that organisation waiting at the airport with all the necessary importation papers.

- **Means of carriage**. How do you plan to transport the equipment to the point of use? Will you carry it as luggage, or box and ship it separately? Both methods have benefits and risks. Carrying the equipment means that (lost luggage aside) you can be confident that both you and it will arrive at the same time. However, as all travellers know, aircraft baggage can be subject to rough handling or careless inspection by customs officers, and thus possible breakages. It also has to conform to airline size and weight limits — and to what you can physically carry! Freight shipping allows for the transport of larger consignments, but shipment needs to be made well in advance of your own arrival.
- Be aware of local **import laws**. If you are bringing equipment into a country, do you have the relevant paperwork? If the equipment is to remain in the country, have you obtained a customs waiver, or will there be duties payable? Follow correct procedure. Failure to do so can lead to difficulties at the point of arrival, and plausibly to the confiscation of equipment. In states where there is a problem with corruption, make sure you do not give customs officials any pretext to extract payments or to make a confiscation.

Your data

The primary aim of your project will usually be to generate digital data. You therefore need to have clear plans for how it will be stored, transferred and protected. Consider the following:

- Where will your primary dataset be held (e.g. on your computer hard drive, camera memory cards or an external hard drive)?
- What is your strategy for backing up your data? Will you make copies to other hard drives or transmit it electronically? If you plan to do the latter, are you absolutely sure that a reliable and sufficiently fast internet link will be available to you?
- Where will you carry out each part of the digitising process? Will everything be done on site, or will you be undertaking processing/export and cataloguing at a later stage? If the latter, how (and when) do you intend to check the product, and what opportunities will you have to reshoot any mistakes?

Politics

Politics may or may not intrude into your project, depending on its subject, scale and its involvement with local government and bureaucracy. The project may be viewed as harmless, eccentric, or could simply slip under the political radar. On the other hand, it may (as many EAP projects have in the past) become enmeshed in local politics. In such cases the actual digitisation has often been the easy part: EAP project directors commonly need to become diplomats and negotiators in order to achieve what is essentially an academic objective.

A few projects have operated in seriously unstable political environments, where work has been severely disrupted, or had to be entirely abandoned. Here, once again, we return to the issue of safety, and circumstances when personal safety outweighs the requirements of the project.

On the other hand, and especially in small polities, the project may bring you into contact with important individuals. Enjoy the experience, and treat this as an opportunity to talk about what you are hoping to achieve, and emphasise how this might be of benefit locally.

- Be aware of local politics, and the dynamic of political or bureaucratic relationships (for example, personal and inter-departmental rivalries; self-interest; corruption).
- Understand how the local bureaucracy works — and the speed at which it may do so.
- Archives (particularly but not exclusively anything modern) could have political currency for both the regime in power and any opposition.
- Try to be aware that you and your project may be being used for external agendas.
- Information (and its control) may be seen as power. Those who hold that mindset may be suspicious of your agenda and resistant to the idea of open access data.
- Expect problems above and beyond the technical. These could well be your greatest challenge, and consume much time.

Archives are not repositories of fond memories. It is likely that the materials you are archiving hold political currency. The materials may be sensitive to the government, or to its opponents, as they have the potential to reveal and remind the world of unwelcome and unsavoury chapters that can tarnish a nation's image. Be sure to have a good understanding of the political climate that you are entering into.

Graeme Counsel, EAP187, EAP327, EAP608, Guinea

Avoid timing your project with a general election, when safety can become an issue. An election also brings the prospect of having to establish relations with a new government administration, its ministers, bureaucracy and ideology, after having gone through this process with the previous administration.

Our place of study was effectively a non-democratic country where the government keeps a close watch on ethnic communities. Projects conducted in ethnic communities therefore must keep a low profile and be sensitive to local politics.

I was dealing with several government departments. In most cases they were only too happy to help, but in a couple there was a concern that this was an attempt to take the section of national archives they manage away from their control, or to make money from other people's archives.

My project digitised court records that were the property of the Registry but which were held in the National Archive. There was no love lost between these different branches of the government or the personnel in charge of them. The project became entangled in these rivalries, and it took a good deal of patient negotiation to obtain access to the records.

> In the course of my EAP projects I have met one head of state and several island governors. All have been friendly, down-to-earth and genuinely interested in our work.
>
> *Andrew Pearson, EAP524, EAP596, EAP688 and EAP794, St Helena and the Caribbean*

> Don't be overwhelmed. In small communities it is likely you will be introduced to very senior people. I had meetings with the Chief Minister and the British Governor. Have at least one good set of clothes for these formal meetings!
>
> *Nigel Sadler, EAP769, Montserrat*

Permissions and Open Access

The relevant local permissions to digitise a collection are a prerequisite of any EAP project, and where possible, should be obtained before a grant application is submitted.

Permission to digitise is also bound up with the question of open access. But, while this concept of accessibility is very much in vogue in academic circles, it is less commonly accepted elsewhere and indeed is a stumbling block that has been regularly encountered during EAP projects.

One of the requirements for EAP funding is that the digitised material is made available online, and for this to be possible, the Endangered Archives Programme needs to receive appropriate documentation. This means the Grant of Permission forms that are on the EAP website will need to be completed and signed. There are two types of form dependent on whether the material is in or out of copyright. Whichever the case may be, EAP only asks for permissions to share the material for non-commercial purposes.

Copyright exists in most countries, and it is the responsibility of the grant holder to know the intellectual property law for the country where the digitisation is taking place. The World Intellectual Property Organisation (WIPO) has a useful website and lists the countries that have copyright law; it includes regional contact details if you need to get in touch with someone.

If the material is in copyright, the grant holder must obtain permissions from the rights holder. EAP requires that this is in the form of a non-exclusive Creative Commons licence for non-commercial purposes (CC BY NC); the form is available on the EAP website. This is the preferred document as it is a simple and flexible licence and allows researchers to understand what they can do with EAP digital material. The 'Grant of Permission Form — CC BY NC' uses clear and straightforward English, but it might still be slightly daunting for a rights holder to be asked to sign a document in a foreign language. It is therefore sensible to translate the relevant forms and explanations that are on the EAP website so that the rights holder understands what they are signing and why.

When copyright has expired, the material becomes Public Domain. With this type of material, there is no longer a rights holder, but EAP still wishes to have an agreement with the owner of the physical material and again seeks a licence so that they can share the material for non-commercial purposes (CC BY NC). This makes it clear that EAP knows that the owner is happy for the material to go online, but it also gives the British Library and other researchers clear guidance as to the copyright status of the material. On this occasion, the 'Grant of Permission form — Public Domain' would need to be signed. Again, it would be wise to translate the form and any explanation so that the owner fully understands what they are agreeing to.

Where permission and access are concerned:

- When dealing locally, be absolutely clear and up-front about the fact that the images will be made openly and freely accessible. Explain clearly what this means.
- Get as many permissions as possible prior to your departure.
- Top-down permissions may not be enough (or even relevant). Very local permissions may be needed.
- Get permissions in writing. Verbal assent may be valueless.
- Carry multiple copies of all your permission letters, as many local collaborators may wish to keep a copy.

In Ethiopia, to do anything beyond pure tourism, one must have official permissions and authorisations. Because we are dealing with ecclesiastical manuscripts we need written approval from both Church and State. Usually, the higher the office (Federal and the Patriarchate), the less effective the authorisation. The final decision is made by the villagers in the local community. One negative voice is enough to halt all proceedings. Even more difficult to accept is that even when an agreement has been made, it can be rescinded after a few hours, or the next day.

Michael Gervers, EAP 254, EAP340, EAP526, EAP704, Ethiopia

Dealing with particular stakeholders can be difficult. The issues that typify workplaces in your home town will also be apparent in your project space, so becoming familiar with Human Resource strategies with regards to dealing with issues in the workplace is recommended. It might sound rather odd, but successfully negotiating your project through an array of bureaucrats with vested interests is a scenario worth considering.

Graeme Counsel, EAP187, EAP327, EAP608, Guinea

Some of the manuscript owners did not fully understand the preservation and scholarly purposes of the project. In such cases, the project team needed to spend time convincing the manuscript owners to allow them to photograph the manuscripts.

Hao Phan, EAP698, Vietnam

My issues with particular individuals were dealt with by seeking advice from trusted stakeholders. I discussed the problems, the lies, the obfuscations, the pretexts to get money. 'Local' solutions were thus offered, and often these were appropriate.

We faced unforeseeable delays and obstacles at almost every step of the way, waiting for months to even get permission from the Central Library to serve as our local host institution. In the case of one participating institution, even after receiving written permission to access and digitise a collection, they did not give us physical access to the collection till almost a whole year after we received the permission.

The biggest disappointment was the en masse withdrawal of a family archive we initially persuaded to work with us. It is difficult to see how we can overcome the basic fear these families seem to share of the political repercussions to themselves of making their private holdings publicly available. However, we also faced a lot of resistance from institutions who were afraid that digitising their collections and making them available at the Central Library would make their own collections redundant and reduce the incentive for potential visitors to come to their institutions. These kinds of attitudes are a real obstacle to digitising and disseminating endangered materials in our country of work.

Obtaining permission from the Government to document the paintings was very difficult and even with the permission, a lot of restrictions were placed upon us. The Hindu Religious and Charitable Endowments Department of Tamil Nadu Government (HR&CE) and the Archaeological Survey of India (ASI) are the controlling authorities of the Hindu temples and monuments of Tamil Nadu. Even though we obtained permission from them, in the case of a particular temple it was very difficult to enter with our equipment because the temple is under the control of local police; we had to wait to get the permission from the official in charge on a daily basis by writing fresh letters and attaching ID proofs.

N Murugesan EAP692, India

Local liaison and partnerships

Local liaison is a core element of EAP projects and is an absolute essential on many levels. At its most basic, this simply involves dialogue with the owners of the materials to be digitised. More commonly, contacts are much more substantive and many projects have been enriched by engagement with local organisations and people. Some points of consideration are listed below, and the subject is also integral to some of the other themes that follow in this chapter, concerning communication, staff and outreach.

- Choose who you trust. Try to do this by obtaining several local perspectives.
- You are an incomer, maybe a 'guest'. Behave tactfully and respectfully, and watch what you say!
- Keep a sense of perspective: the project may be central to you, but you are not the centre of other people's worlds. They have everyday concerns, against which the digitisation of manuscripts may seem unimportant and completely abstract.
- Local problems have local solutions.

Managing expectations

From the outset, and throughout the project, it is important that the scope of your project is clearly understood — both in your own mind, and in communication with others. Managing expectations has to be done from the start and is key to building and maintaining trust.

- Be clear about the aims of your project and how you will achieve them.
- Be equally clear about the limits of your remit — in other words, what you won't be doing.
- Do not make promises you cannot fulfil.
- Where applicable, emphasise local responsibility for the care and curation of the materials. Some projects arrive to find the expectation that they will solve all problems of storage and long-term conservation. Equally, in some former colonial possessions,

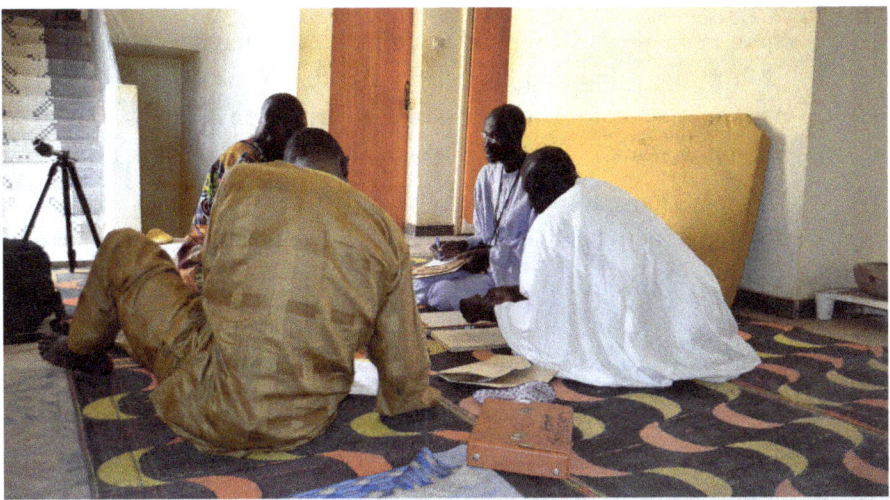

Figure 43. EAP334, Digital preservation of Wolof Ajami manuscripts of Senegal. Photo © Fallou Ngom, CC BY 4.0.

There may be many obstacles, unclear processes and 'ways of doing things' that will be very unfamiliar. These can take up a good deal of your energy, and while reflecting on how to address them is very important, it is also of benefit to discuss the issues with trusted local friends […] Local solutions to local issues can be revealing and appropriate, and sharing problems also helps to limit the stress.

Graeme Counsel, EAP187, EAP327, EAP608, Guinea

Keep your opinions to yourself. This is especially true in small communities. Be aware that if you make a critical comment about somebody, there is a good chance they are a relative or friend of the person to whom you are talking!

Availability of the people was another issue. Most of the people were farmers so it was difficult to meet with them when they had to go for cultivation or harvesting. In such times we had to go to meet with them very early in the morning to at least get the permission to photograph the manuscripts.

Stephen Morey and Poppy Gogoi, EAP373, Assam

there is a belief that the old imperial powers have an obligation to fund the protection of records that they generated. This is a particular issue for projects in former British possessions, due to the connection of EAP to the British Library.

- ☐ You may 'inherit' the legacy of past failures, including promises deemed to have been broken by other incomers.
- ☐ Equally, you may be met by complete mystification! What may be obvious to you can be quite novel to others. In such instances, be prepared to explain your work from first principles, including why it has any value.

> In forming contracts with the international partners, we tried to be specific about the outcome of each project. In most cases, we specified the quantity of digital objects that the project partners were expected to submit. We also included a timeline for each project.
>
> *Hao Phan, EAP698, Vietnam*

> It is good to have an overview of the expectations of the people from the project and to know if they are happy with what is being done.

> We showed them the metadata that we were preparing to convince them that proper record of the manuscripts will be maintained. This was to assure them that their names and family details are being recorded as owners of the manuscripts and that we are not engaged in any kind of business using the manuscripts.
>
> *Stephen Morey and Poppy Gogoi, EAP373, Assam*

The project's most tragic find was several earlier instances of chiefly families loaning their historical documents to historical researchers, only to never have these documents returned. This malpractice at times made our own project difficult, as from the start we entered a toxic situation where our team of genuine and honest researchers, following a strict code of research ethics, were immediately suspected, thanks to the misdeeds of earlier 'researchers'. Families were put at ease not only by the EAP's policies of not removing materials from custodians but also by the very name of the British Library.

Kyle Jackson, EAP454, India

There was a sense that 'this had all been done before without success'. I was regularly told that every project with the archives had either failed or eventually lost momentum. This meant there was already doom and gloom about this project's potential for success.

There also seemed to be a belief that 'someone else would fund the archive development' and not the local government. It was difficult to convince the local departments who managed the archives that this was not going to happen, as was trying to get them to understand that the archives needed better care and greater public access.

Be sure also to teach the abstract and historical reasons why preserving this data is so important. Once your partners understand this, they will be more likely to be consistent and to persevere through longer projects.

David LaFevor, EAP843, Cuba

The lack of face-to-face interaction might create misunderstandings or delay the project. It is thus important to include a travel budget in an international collaborative project to fund meetings in person between the project directors, preferably at an early phase of the project. Communication between the project partners becomes much more effective after such a meeting.

Hao Phan, EAP698, Vietnam

With email having become the main mode of communication at workplaces in the Western world today, it is easy for us to forget that many people in other parts of the world still prefer to communicate by phone or in person.

Hao Phan, EAP698, Vietnam

Some of the locations have been very remote; Quibdo, Chocó (Colombia) was one of the most difficult to reach […] Working in Cuba is always a challenge given the rudimentary communication infrastructure and political difficulties for foreigners who wish to conduct this type of work. The Brazil projects have also presented a number of difficulties stemming from remoteness.

David LaFevor, EAP843, Cuba

After training staff and volunteers I was then available via email, Skype and other internet forums during the three month Pilot Project to help and advise when necessary.

Nigel Sadler, EAP769, Montserrat

All of the problems mentioned were effectively solved by the project team who were patient, persistent, and flexible. The key in dealing with these problems was the fact that the project team included two scholars of Cham ethnicity who are highly respectable people in Cham communities. Other members of the team are also Cham who speak the Cham language and understand Cham culture.

Hao Phan, EAP698, Vietnam

Communication

Good communication is critical, but achieving it is far from straightforward. There is no 'one size fits all' method of dialogue, and different cultures operate differently. And, while modern technology is the default in the Western world, it may be neither practical nor effective in other places.

- Establish a clear structure within the project team. Who is in charge? Who should be issuing instructions? And, for the people on the ground, who is their line manager or first point of contact?
- Email is the common medium for business communication in the Western world, but this is not always the case elsewhere. Face-to-face meetings are often preferred or, failing that, conversations on the phone. Problems that are seemingly intractable often evaporate when you deal with somebody in person.
- If you do not speak the local language(s), make sure that the project engages somebody who does. Such people will not only help with the practical issue of dialogue, but will also understand the cultural dynamics of communication in that society.
- When dealing with local stakeholders, hold as many face-to-face conversations as you can. Dialogue often becomes much harder and less efficient once you are at a distance.
- If managing staff remotely, set up an effective method for long-term communication.

> Although it seems obvious, sometimes we tend to forget that people of different cultures communicate in different styles. A straightforward message from the perspective of an American may be perceived as insensitive by a person from Southeast Asia. We indeed came across a misunderstanding situation with a project partner when trying to urge them to meet the project deadline. When we sent the project partner an email informing them what might have happened with the funding if the project deadline was missed, it seemed that the partner interpreted the message as a threat to eliminate the funding and reacted quite negatively.
>
> Hao Phan, EAP698, Vietnam

Staff and their management

Many EAP projects work with local staff, who often become crucial to their success. The post-project legacy of knowledge and skills is a long-term outcome of great value. However, staff management can be complex, and problems can be exacerbated if you are attempting to run the project remotely through local operatives.

- ☐ Think very carefully about the wages you are paying. Local wage rates can often be extremely low and a minor part of your overall budget. As you train somebody they may become more employable in other walks of life. Do not lose talented staff over the matter of paying a few extra pounds per day.
- ☐ Despite your best efforts you may still lose staff. Design your training to 'cascade' (i.e. local-to-local) after your departure.
- ☐ Delegation of tasks has to be based on your view of staff competence. In terms of skills legacy, and also because it reduces your own burden, one should ideally delegate as much as possible. However, repairing mistakes or shoddy work takes a disproportionate effort. Regularly review the division of labour over the course of the project.
- ☐ Create strong line-management arrangements, through which you retain authority, and in which everybody knows who is answerable to whom. Have a single person responsible for training and providing subsequent advice: avoid the opposite situation, where multiple people give contradictory advice.
- ☐ If managing staff remotely, set up a system of regular progress reports, and keep lines of communication open. In this way you can stay on top of the project, while the staff won't feel isolated and cut adrift.
- ☐ Keep a close eye on the digitised product that is being generated. Do so regularly, so that any technical mistakes are not replicated over multiple documents and any laxness is seen quickly.
- ☐ Consider a means of 'leverage' for local staff. How can you avoid a situation in which you become totally reliant on them, but without any control over when they work or the quality of the product?

This might be through control of money — for example by paying retrospectively on submission of satisfactory work. Alternatively, consider seconding staff who are employed by local government: these will have a line manager who is 'on the spot'. At the end of the day, it is a balancing act. You must trust your staff, whereas a lack of faith, financial ransom or overbearing management will be potentially toxic to the working relationship.

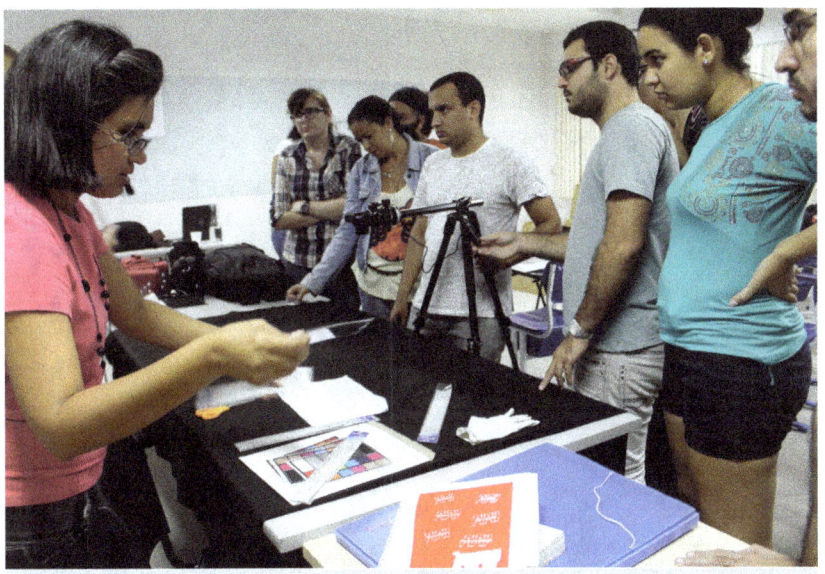

Figure 44. EAP627, Staff training in Paraíba, Brazil.
Photo © Courtney Campbell, CC BY 4.0.

Having a local team that can carry out the work effectively is essential for the success of an EAP project. Members of the project team should include people who belong to the communities that possess the target materials. These team members know best how to work with people in their communities and can overcome many challenges that might be very difficult for an outsider to solve.

Hao Phan, EAP698, Vietnam

The team must include at least one person who is highly proficient in the use of technology. This person will ensure the work carried out meets the standards of EAP and help the team deal with emerging technical problems while working in the field.

Hao Phan, EAP698, Vietnam

I trained several people on how to use the equipment, how to digitise archives in the most effective way and how to handle the archive material to safeguard it. Some of these people have now trained further people to help in the continuing digitisation work post-project.

Nigel Sadler, EAP769, Montserrat

We wrote detailed 'process notes' as part of the training programme. These notes allowed the local staff to have material that reinforced their training, and which acted as a point of reference for anything about which they were unclear. It also allowed them to train others in a correct, structured fashion after our departure.

Andrew Pearson and Ben Jeffs, EAP596, Anguilla

Recently we have had to redo several family collections because the images were too small. Such mistakes are frequent because the locally trained staff are still not totally computer literate and sometimes do not know the difference. Despite repeated training sessions such mistakes occur and the digitisation needs to be extremely closely monitored.

Do not trust entirely that people are doing their job: check and recheck!

> I was amazed at the high level of technical understanding of digital systems that some of the quite young employees had. We learned from this 'digital youth'.
>
> *Martin Jürgens, EAP086, EAP177, EAP326, Laos*

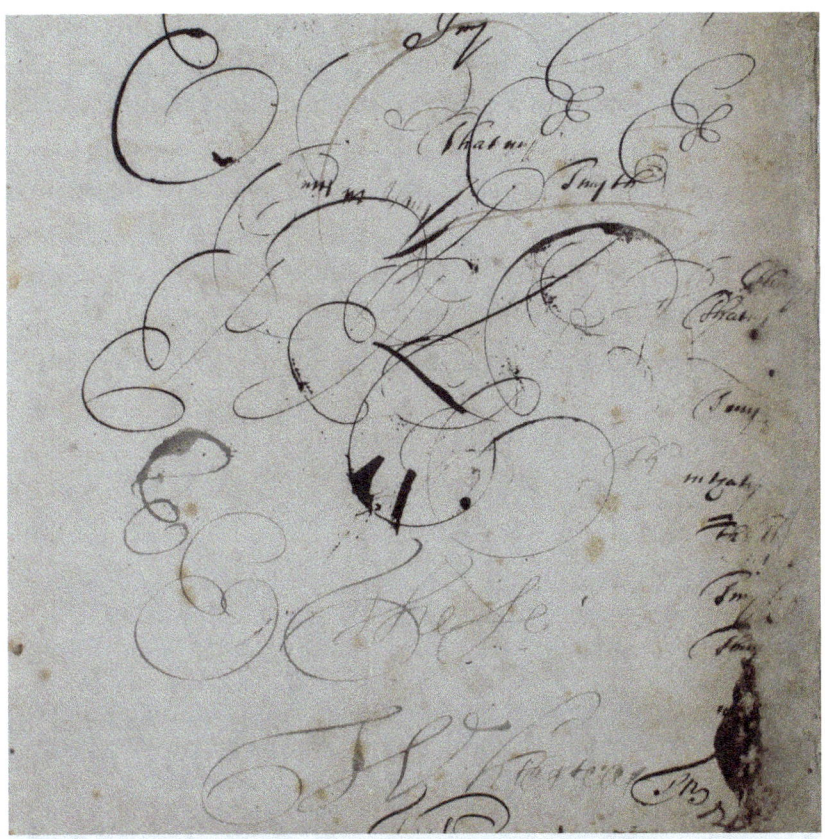

Figure 45. EAP524, Historic doodles.
It is not only modern staff who have the potential to become bored and distracted, as evidenced by this seventeenth-century East India Company document from St Helena. Photo © Andrew Pearson, CC BY 4.0.

Money

Money — and financial management — lies at the heart of the project. As many grant holders have found, however, it is often one of the most difficult issues to deal with. It is also potentially one of the most stressful, particularly when parting with substantial sums of money to third parties.

- Keep detailed records of all spending, no matter how trivial. If you do not record them, small unreceipted expenses may ultimately add up to sizeable 'gaps' in your accounts.
- Update your accounts regularly. Do not return home with a huge bag of receipts and expect to remember every detail of the amounts spent, and on what!
- Obtain receipts for as much as possible. If necessary, carry your own receipt book and ask vendors to fill it out.
- Be aware of the accounting requirements of your host institution. If you do not conform to these, you may find you cannot claim

> While there were many who were enthusiastic about the project, there were some key individuals who were set on frustrating its progress at every opportunity. On more than one occasion I was lied to; there were pretences such as equipment not working or the necessary permission to archive particular materials had not been given, an auxiliary room with project materials was said to 'not exist', and the huge archival task I had in front of me was often dismissed as being impossible to complete. I could not fathom this recalcitrance and obstructiveness (and often, rudeness), until I came to the conclusion that my project did not offer certain individuals sufficient financial incentives. I surmised that the archival collection had remained unarchived for so long, even though specific equipment and personnel had been assigned to the tasks, due to key managers waiting for the 'big project' to come along, with a lucrative budget to match.

for everything you've spent and could end up personally out-of-pocket. This is particularly true in respect of small unreceipted outlays while travelling.

- When transferring large sums to third parties, make sure that there is a clear audit trail. Write or email to inform them that the funds have been transferred; ask that they confirm receipt.

- The vast majority of people with whom you deal will be honest and scrupulous. However, be aware that corruption does exist and in some places is endemic. Where this is a concern, make sure you understand as much as possible about the situation you are dealing with. Again, having an audit trail is critical.

- Foreign money transfers might well be new to you and parting with large sums by 'Forex' may be stressful. At the most basic level, you may not be confident about the transfer process: am I doing this right? have I been given the correct account details? More fundamentally, as noted above, you may be worried about losing the money to a potentially corrupt individual or system. In both these scenarios, consider an initial 'test' transfer. Make sure the funds arrive safely and are correctly assigned. Similarly, rather than sending a single lump sum (e.g. for staff wages), send a series of incremental payments, thus minimising your risk.

- As in so many other aspects, seek local advice and where possible draw on the experience of others who have worked in the same region or country.

> A major cause of disagreement often concerns money. In order to avoid any misunderstanding, a written contract should precede any exchange. Any financial agreement should be written down and signed by all parties concerned, including witnesses.
>
> *Michael Gervers, EAP 254, EAP340, EAP526, EAP704, Ethiopia*

The manuscript owners proved extremely hesitant in letting us photograph the documents in the beginning, while the local administration saw the project as a form of theft. There is still a belief in town amongst some that when the EAP are digitising they are selling the images for a lot of money and that hardly anything trickles back to the manuscript owners.

If you are anything other than an Ethiopian, you will be considered wealthy, hence be prepared for constant demands on your pocket. At the same time, you will be warmly appreciated if you leave tips for the chamber maid, the bell boy and the many other workers with whom you come in contact who subsist on meagre earnings. Your long-term driver should also be recognised for keeping you alive. On the other hand, there is no need to tip at the petrol/gas station, or in taxis. In restaurants, 5% is enough.

Michael Gervers, EAP 254, EAP340, EAP526, EAP704, Ethiopia

Our project's hardest lesson came from financial stewardship. The transfer of large sums of money into official accounts does not mean that officials will act honestly, and this is particularly dangerous in regions where such large transfers are common, and in which the disparity between wages and the bulk transfer is large. Certain politicians and several local corporations are notoriously corrupt. An easy-money ethos seems, tragically, to have somewhat crept into state-run universities as well.

The mistrust of our intentions is still something we have to deal with daily. The fact that we offer a small payment per day for the manuscript owners while we are working on their documents does help.

Do not equate a business relationship with friendship. If you entrust property of any kind to a local, be sure to have the agreement about its return in writing and signed by all parties, including witnesses.

Outreach and publicity

This section concerns peripheral activities that may occur: local liaison, outreach, and publicity. These are practically useful to the project, but are also highly rewarding. Indeed, many grant holders have found this to be the highlight of the project. Grant holders have engaged with schools and local societies, while others have reached out into the broader community. When carrying out this outreach, it is important to be even-handed with competing media outlets.

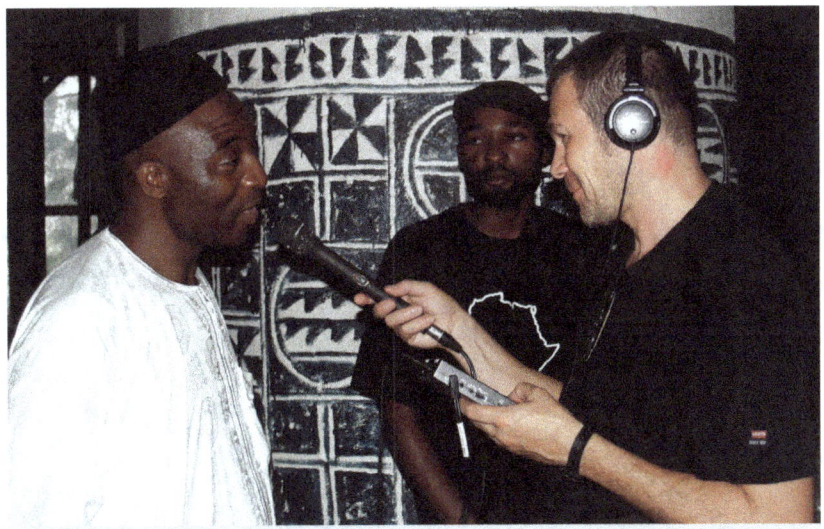

Figure 46. EAP051, BBC World Service radio programme on the importance of Bamum manuscripts, Cameroon.
Photo © Konrad Tuchscherer, CC BY 4.0.

Publicise, publicise, publicise. The mission of the EAP is inherently attractive, and even more so amongst more localised people who are intensely interested in their historical identity or identities. Local universities and colleges jumped on every offer we made to teach their undergraduates about our digitisation project and the 'future of history'.

Kyle Jackson, EAP454, India

Get involved with local events if possible, even if they don't relate to your project. They will provide a great chance to not only promote your project but also to meet people who might be able to help. I was taken to a lunch on my first Sunday but on the way back the driver took a detour to a friend's house where there was an informal drinks party going on. I ended up talking with the committee members of a local organisation who were happy to recount their experiences of growing up in Montserrat. These same people then kept turning up at formal meetings so we were able to talk about lots of things.

Nigel Sadler, EAP769, Montserrat

The most surprising achievement was that following a presentation to the town council, we received donations of numerous boxes of materials from private collections. These included the entire collection of Mariano Sendoya, author, historian, and former mayor of Caloto. This collection has not yet been inventoried, but contains both original archival documents as well as unpublished manuscripts by Sendoya. The other donations were mostly by members of a now defunct historical society. Some of these were from private collections, while others were materials that were taken from the Caloto archive in 2004 after a town employee intentionally set fire to the archival collection, which was in complete disuse.

Thomas Desch Obi, EAP650, Colombia

As a part of our search for privately-held documents we held a 'digitisation day', hosted by the National Library. The event was publicised on radio and in the newspapers, inviting local people to bring in any family documents or photographs that they would like to share. There was an excellent response and, amongst much ephemera, there was some interesting and unusual material. The collection that sticks in my mind belonged to Trevor Davis (alias 'Ras Bucket') an athlete who had competed for his nation at regional and world championships. He brought in photographs and newspaper clippings that spanned his whole career. We photographed these, and the images are now part of the island's archive. Practically none of our digitisation day related to our core project scope, but as means of engaging public interest and showing what we were doing, it was invaluable.

Andrew Pearson and Ben Jeffs, EAP596, Anguilla

The project should also focus on the benefit of the community. The support of the community is very necessary in the smooth running of the project and this is possible only when they realise that they are also going to benefit from project work.

Stephen Morey and Poppy Gogoi, EAP373, Assam

Make as much use of local media as you can. The EAP project in Montserrat was covered in the local newspapers before and after my visit to Montserrat and I also took part in a radio interview to outline the work and answered queries from listeners. I also got invited onto another radio show to talk about the First World War research I had done on Montserrat which allowed me again to promote the EAP and the possible uses of archives.

Nigel Sadler, EAP769, Montserrat

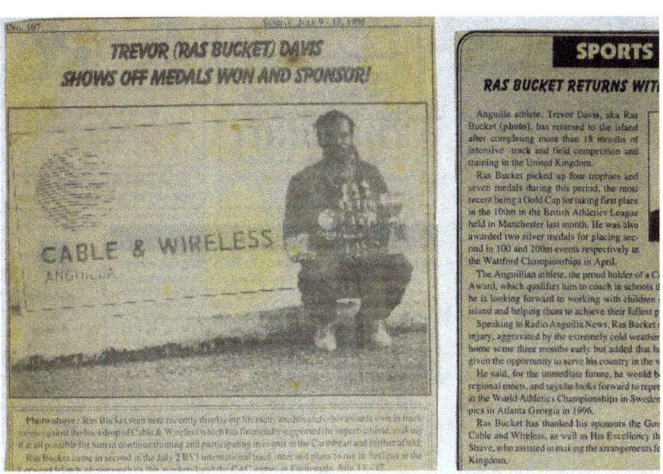

Figure 47. EAP596, Newspaper cuttings photographed as part of the Anguilla EAP's 'Digitisation Day'.
Photo © Andrew Pearson, CC BY 4.0.

Conclusion

Jody Butterworth

The Endangered Archives Programme has had projects around the world from Armenia to Zanzibar. News of the Programme has even made it to the most remote inhabited island of Tristan da Cunha, which has had exceptional issues all of its own with only nine shipments to the island a year and low broadband speeds, making it impossible to send sample images to the EAP office for approval. However, despite the various difficulties that each project has had, the fact that we now have over six million images online is a testament to the successful outcomes of the projects which have been supported so far. The sorts of locations where digitisation has taken place have included desert oasis cities, remote mountainous villages and faraway islands; some of the EAP teams' experiences have been unique, while others have shared common elements.

We hope you will have found the information in these pages useful. You now have all the tools at your fingertips to embark on a digitisation project of your own. You will realise that to plan and undertake a project is no easy task; the preparation, scheduling and organisation must be done a long time in advance. No matter how well prepared you may be, you may face unexpected setbacks, but hopefully the advisory quotations and vivid images from past project holders (who we fondly refer to as the 'EAP Alumni') will inform and inspire you. With any luck, they will help you realise that even in unconventional situations and with sometimes seemingly insurmountable problems, ingenious solutions can be found.

You may have already come to the conclusion that a digitisation project is feasible and achievable and is no longer the daunting prospect it might have been. Perhaps, however, it is important for us to stress the personal rewards you might receive if you choose to go on such an exhilarating journey and it seems fitting that the last words of this publication should be written by an EAP grant holder.

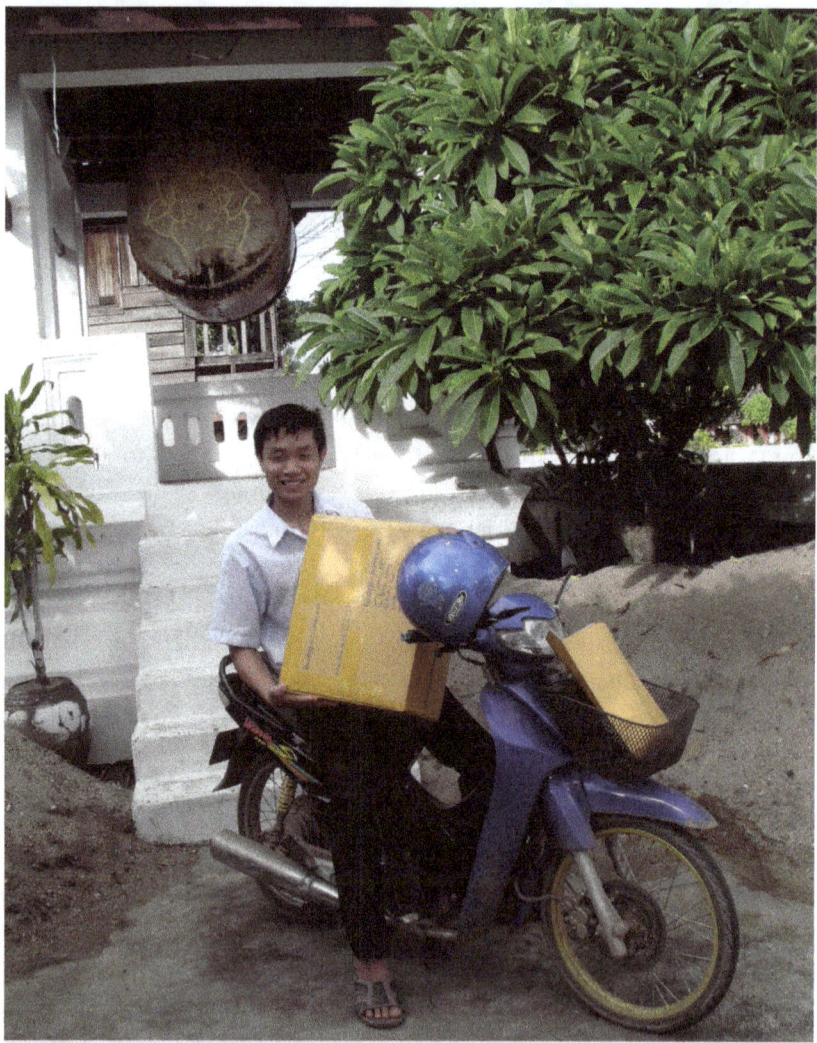

Figure 48. EAP177, Delivering the goods: hard drives ready for postage from Laos. Photo © Martin Jürgens, CC BY 4.0.

EAP051 changed my life — forever. Today I am a different man and scholar than I was only a few years ago. As a result of my time on the ground and work in our EAP project a window has opened to a whole new world of knowledge that was previously impenetrable to me. The world I speak of is a long-forgotten world in the Cameroon Grassfields, a world far away in time from its same location today. It is the Bamum Kingdom, as it once was, long ago, its voice coming alive to me through marks on crumbling paper 100 years old. Imagine a religious epiphany combined with the eureka moment of discovery, for that can only describe the feeling I had when I read a private letter from King Njoya to his closest friend, Nji Mama, as Njoya lies on his deathbed, far away from home, in exile. I collected that letter and I am the first person to read it apart from its original recipient some 76 years ago. It made a difference that I deciphered the characters of the Bamum script myself, written in the dying king's hand. It made a difference to me that I read and understood its message in its original language, Bamum (Shupamom). It made a difference to me that I was the one who unscrambled Njoya's dating cipher to identify when it was written. I experienced that sense of illumination 500 times during our project work. My time collecting, organising, copying, and exploring Bamum documents has armed me with an ability I never dreamt possible. I know every inch of the literate legacy left behind by the Bamum people — not that I have read and understood it all (far from it), but that I know where to find it. Today I am fluent in both the Bamum script (and functional in many of its archaic variants) and the Bamum language. The stage is set for the remainder of my career, which entails probing the documents as a historian, using them to write a Bamum history, which includes an insider perspective based on the written records left behind. For the historiography of Africa, this is a rarity; the possibility of utilising first-hand written records of Africans in the form of an original script, to reconstruct history.

All of the men and women who have been involved in the EAP work feel they have been involved in something truly monumental (and all have been publicly recognised by the Bamum King for this work). But the Archives Du Palais Des Rois Bamoun is more than a monument to me; it represents a lifetime of work ahead, tapping into evidence never before consulted by scholars.

Reflecting on my EAP experience, it was never easy going. We worked long hours around the clock, which had a physical and mental toll. There were the long periods of separation from my wife and children while I was in the field, which were lonely for all of us. I suffered from bouts of sickness ranging from dysentery to malaria, lost significant weight, and was arrested on two occasions by corrupt military police (both times the Bamum King coming to my rescue). Looking back, though, I would never airbrush these experiences from my memory, as they made me a stronger person.

I have only good memories. We worked together as a team, behaving like brothers to one another, all working toward a common goal that we all believed in (and continue to believe in). We worked under the patronage of a king who supported our work. The king came to my aid when I needed it, welcomed me into his home, and at the end of my time in Foumban awarded me with one of the highest ranks in the kingdom for my work on the EAP project (the title of 'Nji'). My relationship with the Bamum Kingdom will only grow stronger…

Konrad Tuchscherer, EAP051, Cameroon

Further resources

Project surveys and outcomes are regularly uploaded to the EAP website, so do browse through the various project pages there: https://eap.bl.uk/. They will help you when planning a project of your own.

Useful downloads

Hill Museum and Manuscript Library downloadable resources (on topics including studio set-up, photography tips, daily steps, camera manuals, software tools etc.): http://www.vhmml.us/Resource/Downloads/

Preservation Advisory Centre guidance booklets on a variety of helpful topics, including: salvaging library and archive collections, moving a library collection, preserving photographic material, managing pests, damaged books, understanding and caring for book bindings, general preservation etc.: http://www.bl.uk/aboutus/stratpolprog/collectioncare/publications/booklets

British Library Collection Care videos for handling items: http://www.bl.uk/aboutus/stratpolprog/collectioncare/publications/videos/index.html

Other reading

Bülow, A, and Ahmon, J, 2011, *Preparing Collections for Digitization*. London: Facet Publishing in association with the UK National Archives.

Kominko, M, 2015, *From Dust to Digital: Ten Years of the Endangered Archives Programme*. Cambridge: Open Book Publishers. https://doi.org/10.11647/OBP.0052. Available to read online and as a PDF download.

Glossary

APS: Advanced Photo System.

APSC: APSC (Advanced Photo System type-C) is an image sensor format used in many high quality digital cameras, including DSLRs. The actual sensor size varies between manufacturers but the sensor area is commonly 40–45% of the area covered by a full-frame sensor. Many APSC cameras have their own range of dedicated lenses but can also use lenses designed for full-frame cameras.

Colour cast: A colour cast is a tint of a particular colour, which is usually unwanted, and which affects the photographic image. Certain sources of light can cause digital photographic files to exhibit colour casts. For example, evening and early morning sunlight may give an overall warm orange-red cast; daylight shade may give a cooler blueish cast, and neon lighting a greenish colour cast. In general, the human eye does not perceive the effect of such variations in colour temperature, because our brains compensate for different light sources. Mixed lighting sources of different colour temperatures cannot be easily compensated for and must be avoided.

Colour temperature: Colour temperature is a measure of a light's colour. Cooler colours give a bluish white and warmer colours give a yellow to reddish white.

Copy stand: This is a device consisting of a baseboard and column that holds the camera steadily in place directly above an item being digitised.

DSLR: Digital Single Lens Reflex camera.

Full-frame camera: A camera in which the sensor is the same size as a frame of traditional 35mm film.

Gutter: The inside margins closest to the spine of a book, or the blank space between two facing pages of a newsletter or magazine.

JISC: Joint Information Systems Committee.

Listing: The Listing template is an Excel spreadsheet that contains all the descriptive data that will be imported into the British Library cataloguing system.

Macro lens: Macro lenses are optically and mechanically designed for close-up photography. True macro lenses should focus down to life-size, with a reproduction ratio of 1:1, but several macro lenses on the market only focus down to 1:2. (When working with a 1:1 reproduction ratio, a full-frame DSLR will fill the frame with a subject 24mm x 36mm) Macro lenses are designed with a longer than normal focussing barrel to facilitate very close focusing. They are also optically optimised for close working distances. Most currently available macro lenses can focus to infinity and also provide excellent optical quality for normal photography.

The term macro is used rather loosely. Many lenses and zoom lenses offer a 'macro' setting. This refers to the ability of the lens to focus closely. Although such lenses with a 'macro' facility may focus closely, they often reveal significant problems of field curvature or barrel distortion visible in the image. In contrast, lenses designed specifically for close-up photography minimise these optical problems.

Metadata: In this context it is the descriptive data about the physical items being digitised and helps identification and discovery.

Plastazote: This is a man-made foam that is stable and therefore safe to use when in contact with fragile items.

RAW: A file format, usually proprietary to each camera manufacturer, that stores all the captured image data without compression.

sRGB: sRGB (standard Red Green Blue) is a colour space commonly employed by digital technology, monitors, the internet and in printing. (In contrast, Adobe RGB is a colour space used primarily by the professional photography printing industry. Theoretically, Adobe RGB can represent a wider range (gamut) of colours but demands special software and a detailed understanding of all stages of digital workflow to manage correctly.)

TIFF: Tagged Image File Format. An image file that stores all the data of an image in a 'lossless' format; this allows the file to be smaller than RAW files but more detailed than JPEG images.

Index

altitude (effects on equipment) 17, 83
aperture 41, 47–52, 54–55, 65, 81, 84, 126
archival collections 15–16, 21, 26, 36, 54, 74, 85, 97, 121, 123, 125, 128, 130, 137, 144, 149, 153, 157, 162, 164, 168–169, 175
  preparation for digitisation 27, 34, 122
  quantification methods for 27–29, 33, 141
  reordering of documents within 123

backup 32, 65, 125, 130–135, 144
  principles 131–132
  types of 132–135
batteries 43, 52, 64–65, 74, 79–83, 145
book supports 117

cameras 13, 16–18, 24–25, 32–33, 36, 38, 41–55, 57, 59–65, 67, 69–72, 74–87, 90, 95–96, 103, 105, 109, 126, 128, 131, 136, 145, 147, 175–177
  Advanced Photo System (APS) 46, 61–62, 79, 176
  brands 25, 44, 60, 67
  care of, cleaning 80, 83–85
  essential skills 41, 81
  full-frame 46, 61–62, 67, 80, 87, 176–177
  remote controls 49, 52, 54, 64–65, 79–80, 119, 143–145, 158, 171
  sensors 45–50, 60, 83–84, 95, 176
cataloguing 29, 32, 127, 136–137, 147, 176. *See also* Listing
checksums 130
colour
  colour cast 53, 57, 59, 73, 176
  colour checkers 52, 58–59, 90, 95, 102–103, 129
  colour space 51, 177
  colour temperature 57, 59, 74, 176
communication 19, 154, 158–160
copy stands 41, 64, 67, 69, 72–74
counterfeit goods 82

data management 42, 86
  transfer 134, 147
data storage media 27, 80, 131
  camera memory cards 80–82, 86, 147
  hard drives 45, 65, 81, 83, 86–87, 131, 134, 147
  memory cards 45, 65, 86–87, 131
depth of field 48, 54–55
digital file formats 60
  JPEG 51, 60–61, 177
  RAW 29, 32–33, 44, 51–52, 57, 60–61, 81, 87, 129, 135, 177
  TIFF 29, 32–33, 43–44, 60, 87, 129, 135, 177

digital images 121, 125–126, 128–129, 136–137
  corrections 127, 129
  developing 60, 128–129, 157
  editing 60, 128
  exporting 32–33, 44, 60, 87, 89, 121, 129–130, 135, 147
  naming 43–44, 121, 127, 128, 132
  sequence of/sorting 117, 123, 127–129
documents 27, 30–33, 35–36, 41, 43–44, 50, 53, 55, 59–60, 62, 87, 90, 113–114, 119, 122–128, 130, 135–137, 142, 151, 153, 157, 160, 163, 166, 168, 173
  bound volumes 16–17, 43, 48, 106, 109, 111, 115, 117, 126–127, 150
  handling methods 9, 30, 43, 113–114, 116–117, 126, 130, 147, 175
  housing media 86–87, 99, 117, 119, 126, 129–130
  loose-leaf volumes 116–117
  terminology 118
  transportation of 125
DSLR 41, 45, 47–49, 51, 60–63, 67, 76, 176–177. *See also* cameras

electricity supply 16–17, 43, 74, 78, 80, 82, 87
Endangered Archives Programme 9, 11, 15, 18, 21, 150, 171, 184
  Arcadia funding of 9–10, 15
  image standards 93–111
  Pilot and Major grant schemes 21, 158
EOS Utility 65–66
equipment 10, 13–14, 16–18, 23, 25–26, 28, 30, 32, 36–39, 41–42, 49, 71, 79–83, 85, 87, 89, 93, 136, 144–147, 153, 162, 164
  compatibility 25–26, 62, 86, 144
  insurance 25, 134, 141–142
  kit 69, 73–74, 78–80, 143–144
  specifying 25, 41

transportation 67, 69, 72, 85, 145, 147
trialling of 21, 30–32, 84, 144–145, 165
exposure 41, 45, 47–57, 60, 61, 64–65, 76, 81, 95, 100–101
exposure modes 50–52, 54, 65, 81
  Aperture Priority mode 50–53, 65, 81
  Manual exposure mode 50–51, 54, 65, 81

flash photography 75
focus 17, 25, 41, 45–46, 51–55, 61–65, 81, 85, 93, 96, 99, 104, 113, 127, 136, 169, 177
framing of images 24, 45, 48, 52–55, 62–65, 67, 73, 83–84, 95–96, 98–99, 101–104, 176–177
freight shipping 25, 147

glass plate negatives 16, 78–79, 90, 116
gloves 114, 116

health and safety 141
histograms 53, 55–57, 65, 81

insurance 25, 134, 141–142
ISO 21, 23, 31–32, 47, 49–52, 54, 61, 81, 100–101, 104, 119, 126, 154, 160, 167, 171, 175

labour requirements 27, 30–36
lenses 16, 25, 41–48, 52, 54, 61–63, 65, 67, 79–81, 83–85, 105–108, 129, 176–177
  choice of lens 61–62
  macro 46, 61, 67, 177
  wide-angle 43–44, 62, 108
lights and lighting 41–42, 45, 47–53, 55, 57–59, 63–65, 68–69, 73–74, 76–80, 85, 90, 94–98, 100, 105–107, 115, 119, 126, 176
Listing 9, 29, 136–137, 176
Live View 65, 126
local partnerships 20

metadata 9, 47, 136, 156, 177. *See also* Listing
money 20, 29, 37, 119, 149, 152, 161, 164–166
   10% grant withholding 39
   accounting 164–166
   customs and import duties 39, 147
   exchange rates 37, 38
   financial contingencies 37–39
   financial corruption 147–148, 165
   international transfers 165
   setting budgets 19–20, 25–26, 28–30, 32, 37–39, 87, 158, 160, 164
   setting the budgets 25
   transfers 165–166

negatives (copying of) 78–79

outreach and publicity 167

permissions and open access 9, 10, 21, 30, 148, 150–153, 155, 164
plastazote 96, 106, 108, 177
politics 13, 142, 143, 148–149, 153, 158
project management 16–17
   tracking documents 122–125

scanners 17, 24–25, 41–44, 78, 87–90, 116
shutter 41, 44, 47–52, 54, 64–65, 81, 84, 97, 100, 126
softbox 95. *See also* lights and lighting
sRGB 51, 177. *See also* colour space
staff 11, 16, 25, 32–34, 35–37, 81, 115, 125, 131, 141, 154, 158–163, 165, 167
   management 159–161
   training 158, 160–162
   wages 25, 37, 160, 165–166. *See also* money
   work permits 141

tethered shooting 45, 49, 65, 126
tripods 24, 26, 41, 49, 52, 54, 64, 67, 70–72, 80, 85

viruses 131, 136
   anti-virus 136
visas 141

white balance 52, 57, 59–60, 81, 95, 103
workflow 17, 30, 62, 121, 137, 177

This book need not end here...

At Open Book Publishers, we are changing the nature of the traditional academic book. The title you have just read will not be left on a library shelf, but will be accessed online by hundreds of readers each month across the globe. OBP publishes only the best academic work: each title passes through a rigorous peer-review process. We make all our books free to read online so that students, researchers and members of the public who can't afford a printed edition will have access to the same ideas. This book and additional content is available at:
https://www.openbookpublishers.com/product/747

Customise

Personalise your copy of this book or design new books using OBP and third-party material. Take chapters or whole books from our published list and make a special edition, a new anthology or an illuminating coursepack. Each customised edition will be produced as a paperback and a downloadable PDF. Find out more at:
https://www.openbookpublishers.com/section/59/1

Donate

If you enjoyed this book, and feel that research like this should be available to all readers, regardless of their income, please think about donating to us. We do not operate for profit and all donations, as with all other revenue we generate, will be used to finance new Open Access publications:
https://www.openbookpublishers.com/section/13/1/support-us

Like Open Book Publishers

Follow @OpenBookPublish

Read more at the Open Book Publishers BLOG

You may also be interested in:

From Dust to Digital
Ten Years of the Endangered Archives Programme

Edited by Maja Kominko

https://www.openbookpublishers.com/product/283

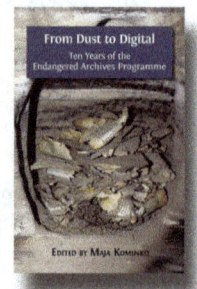

Searching for Sharing
Heritage and Multimedia in Africa

Edited by Daniela Merolla and Mark Turin

https://www.openbookpublishers.com/product/590

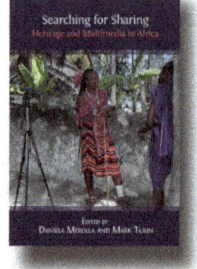

Oral Literature in the Digital Age
Archiving Orality and Connecting with Communities

Edited by Mark Turin, Claire Wheeler and Eleanor Wilkinson

https://www.openbookpublishers.com/product/186

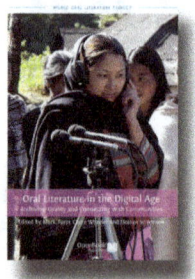

Cultural Heritage Ethics
Between Theory and Practice

Edited by Constantine Sandis

https://www.openbookpublishers.com/product/276

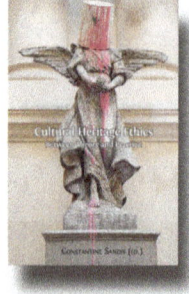